Praise for *Planning for Teaching Success*

"As an alternatively certified K–12 veteran educator, the 2019 Arkansas State Teacher of the Year, and a current professor of aspiring classroom practitioners, I am thrilled to endorse the *Building Your Teaching Toolbox* book series. This comprehensive collection, including *Planning for Teaching Success*, is an indispensable resource for educators at all stages of their careers. The metaphor of a teaching toolbox is brilliantly apt, capturing the essence of how educators continually gather, refine, and adapt strategies to meet the ever-evolving needs of their students.

For new teachers, this series is a treasure trove of practical strategies to fill their newly minted toolboxes, offering them the guidance and confidence to navigate their early years in the profession. For seasoned educators, the series serves as a rejuvenating source of inspiration, providing fresh ideas and innovative approaches to reinvigorate well-worn tools and introduce new ones. The chapters in the book lay a strong foundation for effective teaching. Not only do they help teachers plan for inclusive, collaborative and relevant lessons in responsive learning environments, they also include strategies to help streamline, manage and access the teaching and learning process. The *Building Your Teaching Toolbox* series not only equips educators with a robust array of strategies for teaching students, it also fosters a sense of community among teachers. By sharing and learning from one another, we can collectively enhance our pedagogical practices and ultimately create more equitable and effective learning experiences for all students.

I wholeheartedly recommend this series to any educator seeking to expand their toolkit and enrich their teaching practice. I am convinced that once you delve into this toolbox community, you're going to eagerly look forward to adapting and swapping out these tools and strategies to fit and enhance your own classroom."—**Stacey James McAdoo, 2019 Arkansas State Teacher of the Year; founding executive director for Teach Plus Arkansas**

"Grounded in the work of Grant Wiggins and Jay McTighe, this book is full of useful tips for putting ideas into practice, and adapting to different classrooms and needs. A great guidebook for rookie teachers, it also includes good insights for experienced teachers."—**Susan Kahelin Badger, The Badger Consulting Group; former CEO at Thomson Higher Education and at Pearson, Teacher Education and Development**

"*Building Your Teaching Toolbox* is such a great name for this series. I wish I had this Toolbox when I first started teaching and am so happy I have it now. The structure of *Planning for Teaching Success* has a natural flow and makes veteran teachers more reflective in their practice while laying a strong foundation for newer teachers. It also empowers educators to encourage and support student curiosity. This book is a hitchhiker's guide of practical steps to building a classroom that grows in knowledge, skills, and student agency. You get what you put into your practice, and by using the book *Planning for Teaching Success*, educators will reap the rewards of their efforts."—**Christine Girtain, director of Authentic Science Research, Toms River High School South & Toms River High School North; New Jersey State Teacher of the Year 2022-2023; NABT National Genetics Educator 2022**

Planning for Teaching Success

About *Building Your Teaching Toolbox* Series

We chose to name this series *Building Your Teaching Toolbox* because we think a toolbox is a strong metaphor for becoming an effective educator. New teachers enter the profession with a toolbox that needs to be filled with strategies they can try out and practice to determine which are their "go-to" tools. Veteran teachers often have a teaching toolbox filled with some tools that are well-worn and others that might be in need of revitalizing or updating to make them more efficient and fun to use, and thus more useful for students.

The importance of a well-filled toolbox is not something we take lightly as educators with nearly a half-century of teaching combined under our belts; we continue to revisit our tools to figure out what needs to be updated and consider new strategies to add that enhance our pedagogy. Each district, school, classroom, and child is different, and from year to year, whether a teacher changes schools or not, tools a teacher uses need to be adapted to meet the needs of the new students they are teaching. Therefore, our book series is focused on *Building Your Teaching Toolbox* to support new teachers in developing practical teaching strategies they can adapt for any school context and to support veteran teachers in revitalizing and adding to their already established teaching toolbox.

Within this series, readers will find tried and tested teaching strategies that can be turnkeyed for any school context. The strategies in each book are developed from successful K–12 teachers from across the US and globally. In attempting to create a book that would provide a comprehensive number of teaching tools to fill a teacher's toolbox, we realized one book would not suffice. This led to the creation of the five-book *Building Your Teaching Toolbox* book series that provides 30 strategies in each of four focus areas: (1) classroom climate; (2) planning; (3) instruction; and (4) professional development. The first book in the series provides five core strategies in each of these four areas and each subsequent book is focused on one pedagogical area at a time (book 2: classroom climate; book 3: planning; book 4: instruction; and book 5: professional development).

Having taught and supervised students in so many different school contexts, we knew this book series needed to emphasize how to modify core strategies in multiple ways. Therefore, every teaching strategy throughout the book series includes tips on how to adapt the strategy based on grade level, type of learner, and different school assets and needs like class size, technology, and cultural diversity.

Along with these adaptations, we wanted to be sure that readers could imagine what strategy implementation might be like in their classrooms. Each strategy comes alive through the stories of how contributing teachers have used and adapted the strategies they shared. We also recognize that one great strategy actually requires numerous tiny strategies to effectively execute; so we break down each strategy like nesting dolls where readers will see the overall larger strategy and then more and more details are revealed that will help readers make the strategy their own.

We believe the *Building Your Teaching Toolbox* book series will serve as a practical resource for educators of all backgrounds and experience while also helping to create a toolbox community where we can continue to learn and grow from one another. Thanks for becoming part of that community!

Planning for Teaching Success

30 Practical Strategies for All School Contexts

Jonathan Ryan Davis
Maureen Connolly

ROWMAN & LITTLEFIELD
Lanham • Boulder • New York • London

Published by Rowman & Littlefield
An imprint of The Rowman & Littlefield Publishing Group, Inc.
4501 Forbes Boulevard, Suite 200, Lanham, Maryland 20706
www.rowman.com

86-90 Paul Street, London EC2A 4NE, United Kingdom

Copyright © 2025 by Jonathan Ryan Davis and Maureen Connolly

All rights reserved. No part of this book may be reproduced in any form or by any electronic or mechanical means, including information storage and retrieval systems, without written permission from the publisher, except by a reviewer who may quote passages in a review.

British Library Cataloguing in Publication Information Available

Library of Congress Cataloging-in-Publication Data

Names: Davis, Jonathan Ryan, author. | Connolly, Maureen (English teacher), author.
Title: Planning for teaching success : 30 practical strategies for all school contexts / Jonathan Ryan Davis, Maureen Connolly.
Description: Lanham, Maryland : Rowman & Littlefield, [2025] | Series: Building your teaching toolbox | Includes bibliographical references and index. | Summary: "Planning for Teaching Success: 30 Practical Teaching Strategies for All School Contexts is designed to provide readers with accessible tools that can help them develop meaningful lesson and unit plans in efficient ways"—Provided by publisher.
Identifiers: LCCN 2024027671 (print) | LCCN 2024027672 (ebook) | ISBN 9781475849660 (cloth) | ISBN 9781475849677 (paperback) | ISBN 9781475849684 (epub)
Subjects: LCSH: Lesson planning. | Effective teaching. | Classroom environment.
Classification: LCC LB1027.4 .D38 2025 (print) | LCC LB1027.4 (ebook) | DDC 371.3028—dc23/eng/20240705
LC record available at https://lccn.loc.gov/2024027671
LC ebook record available at https://lccn.loc.gov/2024027672

™ The paper used in this publication meets the minimum requirements of American National Standard for Information Sciences—Permanence of Paper for Printed Library Materials, ANSI/NISO Z39.48-1992.

This book is dedicated to **James Connolly** (1977–2024)—father, husband, brother, son, friend, and teacher. James was inspiring and a "rockstar" to many. His children, Daniel and Lucy, best capture his spirit as funny and kind. All who were lucky enough to meet James were better for having known him.

"You are what you love."—Charlie Kaufman

Contents

	Acknowledgments	xi
	Introduction	1
1	Highlights from *Adaptable Teaching*'s Classroom Climate Strategies	9
	Strategy 1: Yearlong Overview	10
	Strategy 2: Collaborative Planning	12
	Strategy 3: Using Assessment to Guide Instruction	14
	Strategy 4: Inquiry-Based Learning	15
	Strategy 5: Culturally Responsive/Sustaining Teaching	18
2	Desired Results	21
	Strategy 6: Determining Learning Goals	24
	Strategy 7: Thematic Planning	29
	Strategy 8: Connecting Students with Learning Goals	36
	Strategy 9: Connecting with Previous Learning	44
3	Evidence	51
	Strategy 10: Formative Assessments	54
	Strategy 11: Creating Effective Rubrics	60
	Strategy 12: Planning with Feedback in Mind	71
	Strategy 13: Student Choice in How to Represent Learning	79
4	Planning for Instruction	89
	Strategy 14: The Story of Your Lesson(s)	93
	Strategy 15: Incorporating Routines into Your Plans	102
	Strategy 16: Lesson Pacing	110
	Strategy 17: Connecting Skills and Content with Students' Lives and Interests	115
	Strategy 18: Intentional Groupings and Designing Group Work	124
	Strategy 19: Considering Equity and Multiple Perspectives	136
	Strategy 20: Using Learning Management Systems to Organize Your Lessons	146
5	10 Bonus Strategies	155

Conclusion	159
References	161
Index	163

Acknowledgments

We are incredibly grateful to all the teachers who contributed to this book. Our conversations with them were insightful and inspiring, and we are glad to be able to share their planning ideas with you. Each contributor is listed at the start of the strategy that they helped form. We also want to recognize all contributors together, here at the start of this book. We are proud to say that two contributors are a former State Teacher of the Year (denoted with a superscript asterisk next to their name) and one is a former ACTFL National Language Teacher of the Year (denoted with a superscript plus sign next to their name).

Samantha Altman, River Dell Regional High School (NJ), 9th–12th grades
Rebecca Blouwolff,[+] Wellesley Middle School (MA), 6th and 8th grades
Jeff Bradbury, Teachercast (CT), PreK–12th grades
Hallie Brooks, PS 230 (NY), 2nd–3rd grades
Morena Christian, Escuela Campo Alegre (Venezuela), Kindergarten
James Connolly, South Woods Middle School (NY), 7th grade
Kristin DeLorenzo, Francis A. Desmares Elementary (NJ) 1st–4th grades
Kristin Donley,[*] Arapahoe Ridge High School (CO), 9th–12th grades
Alisa Ettienne, Escuelas Lincoln (Argentina), 6th–8th grades
Elyse Hahne, Grapevine Elementary School (TX), PreK–5th grades
Lianne Jones, Westlake Preparatory Lutheran Academy (TX), 5th–8th grades
Amanda Koekemoer, Thomas Paine Elementary (NJ), 5th grade
Kelly DeMarco, Pond Road Middle School (NJ), 6th grade
Shellyann O'Meally, Western International School Shanghai (China), 4th–5th grades
Susan Oppici, Community Middle School (NJ) 7th grade
Kimberly Radostits,[*] Oregon Jr/Sr High School (IL), 8th–12th grades
Heather Rippeteau, Millennium Brooklyn High School (NY), 9th grade
Nita Luthria Row, Bombay International School (India), 5th grade
Akiko Mazor, PS 230 Lower School (NY), Kindergarten
Chris Saunders, Brentwood High School (TN), 9th grade
Rachel Scupp-Jorge, Thomas R. Grover Middle School (NJ), 8th grade
Kathleen Stigliano, Point Road Elementary School (NJ), PreK–4th grades

Kate Sullivan, A. P. Willits Elementary School (NY), Kindergarten
Margaret Summers, Belvedere Elementary School (VA), 5th grade
Eleanor Tixier, FDR Lima (Peru), 7th grade
Erica Unterburger, Matawan Regional High School (NJ), 9th grade
Heather Weck, Harriton High School (PA), 9th–12th grades
Jean Wassel, Rex Putnam High School (OR), 10th–12th grades
Emily Workman, Ed.D., Brentwood High School (TN), 9th grade
Michelle Zimmerman, Renton Prep (WA), 7th–10th grades

Thank you to The College of New Jersey's (TCNJ) School of Education for funding the grant that helped us write this book. Our smart and driven colleagues and friends at TCNJ made this work possible. We are grateful for such a supportive work environment.

Thank you to Druscillla Kojiem, Kerry Rushnak, and Sreenidhi Viswanathan, our research assistants extraordinaire! Your insight, organization, and passion made our writing process smooth and focused, and your research and social media brilliance have helped bring the Toolbox community come to life! These qualities are part of the many gifts you will share with your future students!

Thank you to Donovan Crumpton, the brilliant artist and graphic designer who beautifully crafted this book's cover. A special shout out to Anna for inspiring (and requiring) the teal on the cover, which Donovan integrated so well.

Thank you to the teachers and students who inspired this book! We are humbled by your commitment to teaching and learning, and we hope this book serves as a solid resource for you.

Last, but not least, thank you to our families. Becca, Zola, and Kai—Jonathan is grateful for your unwavering love and support as he navigated long-COVID during the writing of this book; you were his inspiration in being able to write and complete the book as well as getting through a challenging time! Andrew, Anna, and Ben—Maureen appreciates your patience, support, and constant inspiration! We are excited to see how this book can impact and influence our kids' future teachers!

Introduction

WELCOME

Thank you for reading the third book in our *Building Your Teaching Toolbox* series! In this book, we focus specifically on planning. Whether you are a new teacher, veteran teacher, or somewhere in-between, you have probably put a lot of thought and effort into planning engaging and meaningful learning experiences for your students. In this book, you will learn how practicing teachers in diverse school and classroom contexts have implemented successful planning strategies that support learning for *all* students.

WHO WE ARE

As authors and teachers, we represent varied educational settings. We work together as professors of education at The College of New Jersey (TCNJ), which is where we met.

Jonathan's teaching career began as a social studies teacher at Lloyd Memorial High School, a low-income, public high school in northern Kentucky, where he taught for three years. He then moved to teach in New York City for four years in two separate, Title I public schools: Urban Assembly School of Design and Construction (Manhattan high school) and Eagle Academy for Young Men at Ocean Hill (Brooklyn 6–12 school). Jonathan taught global history, New York State Regents and Advanced Placement (AP) US history, government, economics, and a course on race in America. Jonathan was also an adjunct professor for four years at John Jay College, Hunter College, and Brooklyn College, where he taught courses in education, pedagogy, and sociology. During his more than a decade of teaching before becoming a professor of education, Jonathan served as a department chair, instructional coach, and field supervisor for student teachers. At TCNJ, he focuses his research and practice on culturally responsive and sustaining pedagogy—specifically on how to adapt strategies to support the needs of all types of learners in all types of settings. Along with the Toolbox Series, Jonathan has published *Classroom Management in Teacher Education Programs* (Palgrave Macmillan).

Maureen taught English for fifteen years at Mineola High School, a public high school in a middle class, suburban town on Long Island, New York. There, she taught New York State Regents examination support, inclusion, and AP English classes. The range in abilities among her students made her realize the importance of sharing and gathering strong and successful lesson ideas with colleagues. Maureen was also the coordinator for service learning for the New York Metropolitan area and worked at Queens College, Molloy College, and Adelphi University as an adjunct professor of education. She has provided professional development (PD) focused on service learning and literacy across the United States and in several other countries. Along with the Toolbox series, Maureen has published *Getting to the Core of English Language Arts, Grades 6–12* (Corwin); *Getting to the Core of Literacy for History/Social Studies, Science, and Technical Subjects, Grades 6–12* (Corwin); and *Achieving Next Generation Literacy: Using the Tests (You Think) You Hate to Help the Students you Love* (ASCD). Maureen's research and practice is focused on practical strategies and planning that support students' application of knowledge and skills to issues that matter to them.

As teacher educators, our passion, teaching, and research are focused on pedagogical methods to support the needs of both preservice and in-service teachers.

WHY WE WROTE THIS BOOK

There's a great saying, "You plan. God laughs." Whether you believe in a higher power, the sentiment of the saying rings true with most people. If that's the case, why write a book about planning? To answer that question, we share another saying, "Fortune favors the prepared." As supervisors of students entering into this profession, we have certainly seen both of these sayings play out in classrooms. Our teacher candidates sometimes struggle when a plan that they love must be altered. Conversely, they have risen to the challenge of meeting the needs of a variety of students by having well-developed plans to refer to and adapt.

According to the Center for Research on Teaching and Learning (2021):

> To be effective, the lesson plan does not have to be an exhaustive document that describes each and every possible classroom scenario. Nor does it have to anticipate each and every student's response or question. Instead, it should provide you with a general outline of your teaching goals, learning objectives, and means to accomplish them. It is a reminder of what you want to do and how you want to do it. A productive lesson is not one in which everything goes exactly as planned, but one in which both students and instructors learn from each other. (Milkova, 2021, para. 14)

We wrote this book to help share great ideas about and approaches to planning from teachers all over the world. We hope that the tools we share will make your teaching more efficient, supported, and inspired.

WHY THIS BOOK IS FOR ALL TEACHERS

Our work with teachers spans multiple states and countries and connects us with varied school environments. We decided to capitalize on this diversity by developing a book that will help increase the tools teachers can use with their students and help teachers to make mindful decisions about when and how to use those tools based on their students' learning needs.

Research shows that teacher preparation must help preservice teachers develop an array of strategies *and* the ability to reflect on each strategy according to their given setting to plan on how best to proceed (Darling-Hammond, 2015). We believe that this is good practice for *all* educators, regardless of where they are in their careers. This book is intended to both introduce teacher candidates and novice teachers to new strategies and to provide support for the growth and reflective practice of more seasoned teachers.

HOW THIS BOOK IS ORGANIZED

This book is framed by two overarching questions:

1. Which pedagogical strategies have a positive impact on students' learning experiences and the classroom environment?
2. How can we, the researchers, make the intricacies of each pedagogical strategy tangible for novice and experienced teachers working in different settings with varied learners?

For this book, we focus on planning. We created three chapters that align with the three stages of Understanding by Design®: Desired Results, Evidence, and Planning for Instruction. Within each chapter are strategies that you can use to enhance your approach to planning. To make each strategy clear, we detail step-by-step implementation instructions, and to help you envision the strategy further, we provide narratives of the strategy in action. We also quote teachers explaining why they like each strategy.

Because every teacher's classroom is unique, we give examples of how to modify each strategy based on assets and needs of the classroom context, such as technology, cultural diversity, and available time. We also suggest ways to adapt the strategy based on grade level (elementary, middle, and high) and career experience (early-career and veteran).

In our previous books, we have included a section titled, *Considering Different Types of Learners* in each strategy overview. As we wrote this book, we quickly agreed that when planning, any and all adaptations in the following table, should be considered for each strategy.

Considering Different Types of Learners

Students Who Are English-Language Learners				
Provide visuals	Label materials in multiple languages	Translate instructions and materials into students' primary languages	Model expectations and processes	Invite students to write and speak in their primary languages
Students in Special Education Programs				
Scaffold instructions and chunking	Provide positive reinforcement	Schedule breaks	Offer multiple options and formats for students to choose	Minimize distractions
Students in Gifted and Talented Programs				
Encourage students to focus on learning rather than on grades	Celebrate nonacademic successes with students	Provide opportunities for students to take individualized ownership of learning	Challenge students to use more sophisticated vocabulary	Invite students to share how their thinking is extended by hearing new perspectives

In addition to the 20 strategies described in the initial chapters of this book, we include a list of 10 bonus strategies that may be simpler to implement. These strategies are a light lift on your part with a heavy impact on your students.

When reading through strategy descriptions, adaptations, and professional anecdotes and commentary, we hope you feel like a part of a larger community of educators who are eager to share and grow together.

OUR CONTRIBUTORS

We are incredibly grateful to the 30 teachers who contributed to this book. We were fortunate to gather information from educators across 12 states (Colorado, Connecticut, Illinois, Massachusetts, New Jersey, New York, Pennsylvania, Oregon, Tennessee, Texas, Virginia, and Washington) and six countries (Argentina, China, India, Peru, United States, Venezuela). Our contributors represent urban, suburban, and rural settings as well as a range of experience in elementary, middle, and high schools; many of the teachers have also taught in multiple settings throughout their career.

In preparation for the interview process, we asked each contributor to share information regarding their school setting. In the table that follows, we list the percentage of contributors who chose each descriptor as a match for their school. In some categories, you will note that the number of contributors does not equal 30. This is because some contributors believed their school to fall somewhere in the middle of the

Contributors' School Contexts: Assets and Needs

Assets	Needs
My students don't worry about money for basic needs (food, clothing, etc.): 76% (22 teachers)	My students are distracted by concerns about money for basic needs (food, clothing, etc.): 24% (7 teachers)
My students have access to technology inside and outside the classroom: 93% (28 teachers)	My students do not have access to technology in the classroom or at home: 1% (1 teacher)
My classroom population represents a range of racial and ethnic diversity: 68% (17 teachers)	My classroom community is homogeneous in terms of racial and ethnic diversity: 32% (8 teachers)
My class sizes are small: 58% (14 teachers)	My class sizes are large: 42% (10 teachers)
Students consistently attend school: 93% (25 teachers)	Students do not consistently attend school: 7% (2 teachers)
My day is structured to allow time for individual instruction/feedback: 77% (17 teachers)	I rarely have time for individual instruction/feedback: 23% (5 teachers)
My school provides and makes time for quality professional development: 89% (25 teachers)	I do not have access to quality professional development: 11% (3 teachers)
My school values interdisciplinary learning: 88% (23 teachers)	My school does not value interdisciplinary learning: 12% (3 teachers)
I have strong relationships and consistent contact with my students' parents/guardians: 96% (25 teachers)	I have no relationship or interactions with my students' parents/guardians: 4% (1 teacher)
My students want to learn and see that good grades are a result of their learning: 17% (24 teachers)	My students are more focused on good grades, than actual learning: 13% (7 teachers)

descriptors. You can see there is a wide range of assets and needs in the schools that are the "homes" for these teachers, their students, and the strategies within this book.

It was heartening to hear from our contributors that the experience of being interviewed helped them remember and reinforce good strategies. The experience of developing this book reminded us of tried-and-true approaches or informed us of new approaches to use in our own teaching. For this collaboration and inspiration from teacher contributors, we are more grateful than our words can express.

KEY CONCEPTS TO CONSIDER

Understanding by Design

When we think about Understanding by Design® (UbD), we consider the three main stages: Desired Results, Evidence, and Planning for Instruction. Within the following chapters, we will explore strategies that relate to each stage. We use these stages as foundations for planning because of the structure and rationale that they support.

According to Wiggins and McTighe (2005)

> Instead of simply listing the topics taught, a UbD map specifies the big ideas and essential questions that are addressed at various points in the curriculum. . . . Additionally, we propose that a UbD map should include core assessment tasks that all students would perform to demonstrate their understanding of key ideas and processes. (Of course, these tasks would be accompanied by agreed-upon scoring rubrics.) We believe that such curriculum mapping brings conceptual clarity and coherence to the curriculum. (p. 26)

Using UbD for planning ensures a curriculum that is cohesive and logical in helping students progress in their development of knowledge, skills, and dispositions.

Differentiation and Scaffolding

Throughout this book, we discuss how to differentiate planning by considering students' interests, readiness, and learning modalities. Based on what is understood about students, we give guidance on how to plan for appropriate content, process, and products that align with where students are and where you want them to go with their learning.

Scaffolding is when teachers provide support to students as needed and then gradually help students move toward working independent of teacher support. We like the Great School Partnership's (2015) overview of scaffolding:

> The term itself offers the relevant descriptive metaphor: teachers provide successive levels of temporary support that help students reach higher levels of comprehension and skill acquisition that they would not be able to achieve without assistance. Like physical scaffolding, the supportive strategies are incrementally removed when they are no longer needed, and the teacher gradually shifts more responsibility over the learning process to the student. (https://www.edglossary.org/scaffolding/)

For all students, but particularly for students who are English-language learners, in special education programs, and students with low self-esteem (and other nonclassified students), it is important to focus on their strengths and assets and *not deficits*.

Universal Design for Learning

Universal design for learning (UDL) in education is based on the UDL access laws that ensured that all individuals would be able to enter public buildings. This meant the construction of ramps, elevators, and more. When applied to education, this framework "intentionally allows for learner variability and embraces flexibility in the engagement of students, representation of content, and the learner's expression of knowledge" (Lowrey & Classen, 2019, p. 1).

UDL is based on three guidelines that have been outlined by the Center for Applied Special Technology (CAST): engagement, representation, and action of expression. The following table represents the guidelines and beliefs associated with UDL along with their implications for planning.

Guidelines, Beliefs, and Implications Associated with the Universal Design of Learning

Guideline	Belief	Implication
Engagement (the *why* of learning)	"There is not one means of engagement that will be optimal for all learners in all contexts."	Spark students' interest Supporting students' persistence Developing students' self-regulation
Representation (the *what* of learning)	"There is not one means of representation that will be optimal for all learners."	Share multiple forms of information (written, auditory, different languages, etc.) Provide schema and scaffolds to help students' comprehension and transfer
Action and Expression (the *how* of learning)	"There is not one means of action and expression that will be optimal for all learners."	Vary physical access to tools and methods of expression Use goal setting and a plan to progress in developing executive functions

Based on https://www.cast.org/impact/universal-design-for-learning-udl

UDL integrates elements of UbD and differentiation. We recommend using elements of all these approaches throughout your planning.

Balance

Just as you work to make learning accessible to all students, we urge you to make this profession viable and sustainable for yourselves. Teaching is incredibly demanding, and thankfully, incredibly rewarding. That said, to maintain your commitment and enthusiasm for this profession, you must find balance. In yoga, you need to utilize your core in order to maintain a balance pose. This translates well to life in general. Know your core beliefs and values and use them to guide your decision making. Jim Burke (2023) created an excellent planner, at the start of which he shares six commitments:

1. I am committed to the success and well-being of all my students and to their learning.
2. I know my subject well and how to teach it so that all my students will learn, remember, and enjoy it.
3. I am responsible for designing, teaching, and assessing the lessons and learning of all my students.
4. I consider equity and access when designing, teaching, and assessing my lessons and students' learning.

5. I reflect on, analyze, and refine my teaching based on feedback from multiple sources.
6. I participate in and contribute to my learning community at school and the profession at large.

(Burke, 2023, p. 12)

This list provides a strong touchstone for the beliefs that guide how we want to operate as teachers. We also encourage you to remember the why behind what we do. What inspired you to be a teacher? What makes this job so special to you? Having both the how and the why at your core will help you to find balance in this work, even on challenging days. It is also important to remember that while your work matters, your whole self needs to be nurtured and supported as you strive for work-life balance.

Flexibility

Our best advice as you read through this book is that *a flexible life is a happy life*. Although we encourage you to have a large-scale vision for classroom learning, we want you to maintain flexibility with this vision. We suggest that you only make copies of or post materials for instruction a few days in advance because you may need to make changes based on conversations in your classroom or skills that need further development. During a keynote, Grant Wiggins, the codesigner of UbD stated, "Plan . . . [insert dramatic pause] . . . to adapt." Wiggins himself made clear the importance of being open to change based on students' needs.

Final Words

We've structured the strategies in each chapter to be as accessible as possible for teachers from any classroom context through our detailed, step-by-step overviews, teacher narratives, and sample adaptations. Remember, teaching and learning are about trying new ideas and approaches. We want to encourage you to explore new ways to make your classroom an optimal learning environment where you and your students thrive together.

If you have some great stories about how you have used these strategies, please connect with us!

Website: https://buildyourteachingtoolbox.com/
Email: info@buildteachtool.com
Twitter: @BuildTeachTool
Instagram: @buildteachingtoolbox
Facebook: Build Your Teaching Toolbox

Chapter 1

Highlights from *Adaptable Teaching*'s Classroom Climate Strategies

Adaptable Teaching: 30 Practical Strategies for All School Contexts (2022), the first book in the *Building Your Teaching Toolbox* series, includes strategies related to classroom climate, planning, instruction, and professional development. Although *Planning for Teaching Success* focuses exclusively on planning, many strategies in this book build on the classroom planning strategies presented in *Adaptable Teaching*. This chapter provides brief descriptions of the planning strategies from *Adaptable Teaching* and steps for implementation.

For the detailed narratives and adaptations for each strategy in this chapter, check out *Adaptable Teaching*!

STRATEGY 1: YEARLONG OVERVIEW

Creating a yearlong overview begins by using Understanding by Design® (UbD) to align the year's larger learning objectives with the course's map. The overview breaks down how each course unit and lesson build toward achieving those yearlong goals and provides a basic structure and pacing guide for the year. This is a holistic view of the year that frames the way you develop your day-to-day lesson plans. The yearlong overview is not about writing every lesson plan months in advance of teaching; it is about developing a frame for outlining unit and lesson ideas that fit a larger vision of learning for the year.

Strategy Implementation

1. **Create yearlong calendar/template.** Create an academic year calendar template that includes: all school days, school breaks, professional development, school-wide activities, and any other event that will impact your instruction.
   - If available, use an already existing academic calendar template created by your school, district, or somewhere else.
   - Adapt the calendar template to make it accessible for you (e.g., change fonts, highlight).
   - Consider whether you want a digital copy, a hard copy of the template, or both. If digital, add the calendar to a cloud-based system (Google Drive, Dropbox, etc.) so it is backed up.

2. **Get to know course standards and learning objectives.** Identify and examine the relevant course standards (national and/or state) as well as any course-provided learning objectives (national, state, or district). You can use these standards and learning objectives to brainstorm themes for units that become frames for unit plans. Think about how you will:
   - Unpack the language of the standards and learning objectives to make them more accessible for you and your students and to meet the needs of your students.
   - Address the skills and content needs of each student.
   - Ensure your students are able to meet these standards and objectives.
   - Determine which standards are complex and will require that you integrate supports to help your students meet the standards and objectives.

3. **Think backward.** Apply the three stages of UbD (desired results, evidence, and planning for instruction) to determine where you want students to end up at the end of the year and then how you will help them get there. Begin by thinking about the end-of-year goals and then how each unit goal will help build toward the end-of-year goals. Determine:
   - The larger enduring understandings and essential questions you want your students to take away from your class *by the end of the year*.
   - What enduring understandings and essential questions students will need to answer during your *units* to master the larger enduring understandings and essential questions for the year.

4. **Map out curricular units.** Based on your analysis of standards and learning objectives (step 2) and the development of your desired results (step 3), determine which units are essential to teach your class during the year. Then sequence the units on your calendar. Consider:
   - The most logical way to sequence your units to build toward the end-of-year goals.
   - Whether the sequencing of your units makes sense.
   - If the unit sequencing helps your students build their skills and content knowledge from one unit to the next.

5. **Add assessments and align to standards.** Once the units are mapped out on your calendar, determine potential assessments to measure student mastery of each unit's enduring understandings, essential questions, skills, content, and/or dispositions. Make sure to:
   - Integrate both formative and summative unit assessments to align with standards and meet the big ideas for the unit and the year.
   - Ensure your assessment sequencing throughout the year helps support students' skill and content development.
   - Create a diversity of traditional and nontraditional assessments to engage and assess your students.

   NOTE: Although it is great to plan ahead, be ready to adapt your assessments as you get to know your students' strengths and needs.

6. **Add daily lesson topics and outline of activities (lesson plan outline).** The final step in creating your initial yearlong overview is to fill in the lesson *topics* for each day of the year (within the context of each unit) and then *outline* the activities you want to include each day. Ensure:
   - Your lesson topics align with the big ideas for each unit and its summative assessment.
   - The sequencing of each lesson topic supports logical content and skill development.
   - Lesson activities are varied, engaging, and student-centered.

7. **Adapt overview as needed throughout the year.** After the school year begins and you have met your students, it is important to revisit and update the yearlong overview to best support the learners in your classroom. Here are some tips on how to do so:
   - Fix something the minute you have to. If you don't get through something on Monday, you fix the rest of the unit. Typically update it every few days.
   - Adjust the dates and schedule for your yearlong overview based on your students' needs as you learn about new school events, curricular needs, and so on.
   - Make notations in red at the bottom of a page as a note for the next year.

STRATEGY 2: COLLABORATIVE PLANNING

Collaborative planning can take place among teachers by grade level, subject, or teams of teachers who work with the same students. It can include a large group of teachers or as few as a pair of teachers. Some schools block time into teachers' schedules to allow for this collaboration, and in other schools, teachers have to find their own time to coordinate with one another. When teachers engage in collaborative planning, they may be reviewing assessment data, preparing curriculum/instruction, discussing social-emotional or behavioral needs of students, or developing ways to impact classroom, school, and/or community culture.

Strategy Implementation

1. **Find your people.** You may be assigned to a group of colleagues as part of your professional development (PD) plan or nonteaching responsibilities. If not, or if you want an additional collaborative group, consider who is interested in collaborating. This may include groups based on grade level, common students, or common content. You can "sell" the idea of collaborative planning by noting the following benefits:
   - Improved morale due to support and feedback.
   - Better teaching due to multiple perspectives and backgrounds.
   - Insight into students' actions outside your classroom.
   - Alignment among subjects and grade levels.

2. **Set up a time to meet and stick to it!** Collaborative planning may take place daily or, more likely, two to three times per week. To help you stick to the schedule you make, try the following:
   - Find a meeting place that is consistently available.
   - Send out an agenda with the reminder email so people can prepare or consider ideas beforehand. This can be just one line (e.g., Discuss struggling students and bring names) or several items.
   - Invite administrators and support staff such as guidance counselors, social workers, and paraprofessionals. This will streamline their time in sharing information if they can talk to several teachers at once.

3. **Determine roles.** Most collaborative planning teams are fairly casual. Think of a professional learning community (PLC) but much more relaxed. That said, you may want to determine some key roles such as:
   - *Notetaker/Note Poster:* Types up notes or revises materials and then posts to a shared drive.
   - *Scheduler:* Emails reminders of upcoming meetings.
   - *Timekeeper:* Just like students, teachers can get off track, so a timekeeper may be helpful in guiding groups back to their agenda.

4. **Focus on your purpose.** As a group, determine your purpose and then connect back to it in the work you do. Remember, you might amend your original purpose and that is OK! You are evolving as a group. Determine:
   - What you want to do as a group.
   - How your work will support students' development of knowledge, skills, and dispositions.
   - How your work will help the classroom, school, and/or larger community.

5. **Share your work!** When you work with a collaborative group, you push your thinking and expand your productivity. This is worth sharing with others! You might share your work with:
   - Other collaborative groups.
   - Administrators.
   - Colleagues at a faculty meeting or conference.

STRATEGY 3: USING ASSESSMENT TO GUIDE INSTRUCTION

Use formal and informal assessments to guide planning based on students' knowledge, skills, and dispositions (K/S/D). This may be done on a large or small scale with short-term or long-term goals. For instance, you might use a diagnostic assessment that leads to individual learning pathways to support student mastery in topics or use a short, informal assessment at the end of class to determine adjustments for subsequent lessons.

Strategy Implementation

1. **Focus on objectives.** Consider the objectives for the unit and the learning experiences you are developing. Think about:
   - The K/S/D you want your students to develop.
   - How these K/S/D correlate with standards and assessment.
   - How the learning experiences you are designing help students meet or exceed the unit objectives.

2. **Select your mode of assessment.** Decide which assessment(s) will be most useful for you. Consider:
   - What you know about students' K/S/D from prior units' formative and summative assessments.
   - Diagnostic assessments that will hone in on the baseline of students' K/S/D for the unit.
   - Formative assessments that will show growth over time.
   - Summative assessment options that highlight students' K/S/D through varied means.

3. **Assess your students.** Remember that assess means "to sit beside." This is not about earning a grade or a high score. How does the approach you chose enable you to sit beside each student to gather a sense of how they are developing their K/S/D? When you assess, contemplate:
   - The K/S/D that students are developing.
   - The K/S/D that are challenging for students.
   - The ways students have met or exceeded K/S/D objectives.
   - Whether you need to grade the assessment, and if so, how to ensure the grading does not impede authentic student answers.

4. **Plan next steps.** Based on what you learn about K/S/D from all your assessments, create "learning paths," from novice through challenging, to review or practice skills. Learning paths are a series of learning experiences that can be adapted based on students' needs, including video lessons, practice problems with self-assessment, mini-projects, and so on. Support students during two to three days of individual and/or group work to prepare for a larger, full-class activity or project that builds and extends skills. Focus on:
   - How to support students who are struggling.
   - How to extend student learning if students have already met the K/S/D objectives.
   - Where to go next if all students have met or exceeded all objectives.

STRATEGY 4: INQUIRY-BASED LEARNING

Inquiry-based learning starts with sparking students' curiosity to learn about a topic that matters to them. Students engage in research and experimentation to address a question or problem, and they share their findings with peers and teachers. This strategy transfers responsibility from teacher to student. With the understanding that they are supported, students can take risks in their learning, discover patterns and make connections to help them grasp difficult concepts, and explore multiple solutions without the fear of finding *only one* right answer.

Strategy Implementation
Part I: Planning and Preparation

1. **Determine the activity/project's big ideas.** Develop the inquiry activity/project's essential questions, student learning objectives, evidence of student learning, and connections to state learning standards. Ensure:
   - The essence of your inquiry-based activity/project is something all your students will want to do and will find meaning in doing.
   - Your essential questions have multiple potential answers, require deep investigation, and necessitate layers of critical thinking and analysis to answer.
   - The evidence of student learning is authentic and supportive of your diverse learners.

2. **Create an open-ended "problem" to present students.** Based on your essential questions, create an open-ended problem to present to your students. Consider the questions:
   - Is the problem something all students can understand?
   - Is the problem something all students will want to get to the bottom of?

3. **Identify resources and materials needed.** Decide which resources and materials are necessary to make your activity or project happen. Keep in mind which resources and/or materials:
   - You have access to in your school.
   - Your students have access to at home.
   - Are necessary to make the project happen.
   - Would be a luxury to have.
   - Are sharable.
   - Can be reused or repurposed.

4. **Determine method of assessment.** Plan how you will assess or evaluate the work of students. This can be as simple as student reflection, an in-depth rubric, or written or verbal feedback. Determine:
   - What is the best way to assess students for this activity or project?
   - What type of feedback is best to support students for this activity or project?

5. **Write up your activity/project.** Once you have determined your big ideas, created one open-ended problem, and determined the necessary materials, write up your project and break down the steps of the students' investigation. Make sure to:
   - Scaffold the steps of investigation in a way that is developmentally appropriate for your students.
   - Differentiate the project in necessary ways to support the different learners in your classroom.

Part II: Introducing and Executing the Plan

1. **Introduce the activity/project.** Take the necessary time to introduce the activity or project so *all* students are clear about expectations and what to do before they begin. Do the following:
   - Provide "Instructions Three Ways": (1) orally with the whole class; (2) projected or written on the board; and (3) on paper/computer in front of the students.
   - Review the assignment; have students reinforce what they have to do, and answer any student questions.
   - If you have time, give students (once in groups) a chance to discuss the activity or project and develop any additional questions they have to pose in front of the class.
   - Once all questions have been answered, have students begin.

2. **Give students time to explore.** It is important to allow groups space and time to explore the problem on their own with built-in scaffolds and support from the teacher. This can be done in one day or across multiple days. Some strategies include:
   - Prepare prompting/guiding questions for your students.
   - Use work time to conference with groups and individual students.
   - Scaffold or chunk the exploration so students have clear guidelines and targets to support their exploration.

3. **Share and debrief.** Give students time to explain their findings. They can elaborate on what they have found by leading a discussion with a small group or the whole class. This is a great time to engage in critical reflection about where they and their group are in the process of their exploration.

4. **Revise and move toward solution.** Have students take the feedback they received from their peers and revise their work as they move toward their solution to the problem.
   - Provide guiding questions and graphic organizers to support the revision process.
   - Ensure students are relying on analysis of evidence to come up with and support their solution.

5. **Final product.** Provide students with clear expectations for the final product they are producing (rubric or other template). Make sure:
   - The final product reflects the work of the *entire group* and *individual contributions*.
   - Groups share their findings.
   - The whole class engages in debates/discussions around different solutions to the "problem."

Part III: Assessing and Reflecting

1. **Assess individuals and groups.** For any group work, determine how you can assess the group as a whole as well as each member of the group. Consider:
   - Which components of the activity or project reflect *individual* student work that you can effectively assess?
   - What criteria you can use to assess the entire *group*?
   - Whether students should self-assess their *individual* and *group* performance and their mastery of the content and skills?

2. **Critical reflection.** Reflect on the lesson or the project. What went well? What did not go well? Think about what you might want to change if you were to teach this again. Make sure both the *students* and you as the *teacher* can critically reflect on the *process* and *product* of the activity or project.

STRATEGY 5: CULTURALLY RESPONSIVE/SUSTAINING TEACHING

Culturally responsive/sustaining teaching (CRT) takes into account the academic, social, and cultural knowledge that students bring to the classroom. Students' cultures and backgrounds are seen as assets—not deficits—in the classroom. Teachers design the learning environment with students at the center and work to promote equity in the classroom and justice in the world.

Strategy Implementation
Part I: Understanding Who Is in Your Classroom

1. **Recognize multiple cultures exist in your class (at any given time).** Within every classroom, the following cultures exist:
   - *Classroom Culture:* The culture in your classroom that you, as a teacher, must create to make the students feel safe and wanted.
   - *Student Culture:* The culture each student brings from home; their instilled family values and belief systems.
   - *Community Culture:* The norms and practices within the students' community where you teach.

2. **Research students' cultures.** Finds ways to research the cultural backgrounds of each of your students to get to know them better and ensure you don't perpetuate stereotypes. This shows students that you have a personal interest in them. Consider:
   - The most effective way to identify the cultural backgrounds of your students.
   - The best way to learn from your students about their cultural backgrounds (e.g., talking to them; asking them questions; assigning projects related to their culture).
   - What you can read about your students' cultural backgrounds and how you can ensure a diversity of sources in learning about their backgrounds.

3. **Build relationships with and among your students.** Find ways to integrate relationship building (teacher-student and student-student relationships) *during* your class time. Consider:
   - Relationship-building activities you can integrate into lessons.
   - Spaces during lesson(s) that lend themselves to relationship building.
   - Ways to sustain relationship building in your classroom throughout the year.

Additionally, you can *use nontraditional* times for relationship building. Consider:
   - Inviting students to eat lunch in your classroom to talk with them about things not related to school or stopping them in the hallway to do the same.
   - Attending extracurricular activities (it shows you are interested in their life).
   - Listening to students' music, likes, and dislikes.

Part II: Planning for Your Classroom

1. **Create engaging assignments that empower students of all backgrounds.** Use your knowledge of your students' backgrounds to create assignments that celebrate your students' cultures and connect with your students' lived experiences. Make sure to:
   - Connect students' cultural backgrounds with class content.
   - Focus on individuals that demonstrate and celebrate aspects of students' cultures.
   - Find readings and texts that are responsive to the backgrounds of your students.
   - Be inclusive of all your students by discussing multiple viewpoints when certain class texts and topics align more with particular student backgrounds.

2. **Personalize student learning.** Consider student interests, backgrounds, and lived experiences when you develop learning objectives and learning experiences and design assessments to represent student growth.

3. **Ensure class texts are diverse.** Read and study works created by diverse authors and artists. These can be texts that align with your students' cultural backgrounds as well as texts that expose students to unfamiliar cultural backgrounds.

4. **Show and tell.** Regularly bring in artifacts that students can touch and learn about. Encourage students to bring in artifacts to discuss. As Naeem Muse noted, "We are never too old for show and tell."

Part III: Implementing Your CRT Plan

1. **Greet your students.** Stand outside the classroom, and greet each student as they enter the room. Do this on a daily basis to set the tone for your time together. When greeting students, ensure you:
   - View facial expressions and body language to get a quick gauge of each students' mental and physical well-being.
   - Be relaxed, and let the students know that you are happy to see them—especially the student that may be more challenging than most.

2. **Sharing cultural backgrounds/identities.** When integrating assignments and experiences that help students explore their own and others' cultural backgrounds, build in time and exercises that support students sharing their backgrounds and identities with one another. Consider:
   - Which activities allow students to share their cultural backgrounds and identities in a respectful way?
   - How will you prepare the class to share personal information about themselves and learn about others' backgrounds?

3. **Ensure every student is heard.** Every child wants to be heard, so listen to what they have to say even if it seems unimportant or uninteresting to you. This includes:
   - Prioritizing class time for students to share their stories.
   - Letting students tell their story without interruption.
   - Giving constant feedback and responding to their life stories.

4. **Use "we messages."** Using we messages makes everyone feel included and part of a collective community. In particular, with this inclusive way of speaking and addressing the class, withdrawn and quiet students and students whose behavior may be in question are reminded in a gentle manner what is and is not acceptable. We messages also make students accountable for each other's actions, and eventually students will address each other's actions without teacher involvement. We messages include:
   - When explaining something to the class, say, "Today we are going to . . .".
   - If someone does something wrong, say, "We don't do that in here."

5. **Take action against injustice.** Name injustices you see and hear in the classroom, and discuss ways to overcome them (or ways that people have already worked to overcome them). This might include topics covered within your content or when students say or do things that are hurtful, perpetuate stereotypes, or go against the class norms and expectations. When addressing injustices in your classroom, make sure to:
   - Figure out how to address the injustice directly and respectfully.
   - Determine a tangible action against the injustice that will have a direct impact on the lives of your students.
   - Consider which class projects are most effective in connecting classroom content with actions students can take that relate to effect change in their lives.

Chapter 2

Desired Results

In this chapter you will find strategies for determining your desired results and using them to guide your planning. These include:

- **Determining Learning Goals** by using the big ideas, skills, and dispositions you want your students to develop so that a clear plan can be created (Strategy 6).

    The biggest part of backwards planning is knowing what the end is because it allows students the ability to chunk and retain information for longer-term learning of concepts.

    —Jean Wassel

- **Thematic Planning** of lessons and units of study to provide a strong rationale for learning (Strategy 7).

    When we follow a series of lessons day-to-day, it is easy to get bogged down in what we are doing each day rather than taking a broad view and showing how the lessons are connected.

    —Emily Workman

- **Connecting Students with Learning Goals** to make learning more personal (Strategy 8).

    The reality of teaching is that our strategies continue to evolve each year because we must adapt to students and alter plans based on the effectiveness of the previous year and based on who the learners are at the time.

    —Chris Saunders

- **Connecting with Previous Learning** to build students' competence and confidence (Strategy 9).

  > [Students] are actively learning and curious about the connections that we are trying to get them to think about. They engage at a metacognitive level that helps them become agile, creative, and adaptable learners.
  >
  > —*James Connolly*

HIGHLIGHTS

- Learn about working with a team to determine desired results in **Determining Learning Goals** (Strategy 6).
- Explore ways to connect themes across disciplines in **Thematic Planning** (Strategy 7).
- Think about how to vary content so lessons are meaningful and inclusive in **Connecting Students with Learning Goals** (Strategy 8).
- Explore how students can develop toolkits of knowledge and skills in **Connecting with Previous Learning** (Strategy 9).

HOW THESE STRATEGIES MIGHT BE ADAPTED BASED ON TEACHING EXPERIENCE

This chapter is focused on using desired results to guide planning. As you examine the strategies presented, consider how your teaching experience may influence your planning choices. Some advice for both early-career and veteran teachers follows.

Early-Career Teachers

Make it a priority to look at as many possible curricula related to your content as you can. Then connect with colleagues (at your school or virtually) who teach the same material to discuss effective end goals they have used in the past. Use all this information to determine your desired results.

Veteran Teachers

Seek out new ideas and perspectives from early-career teachers on what they see as important about the knowledge, skills, and dispositions related to what you are teaching. Talk with colleagues about your planning areas of strength and how you can build on your previous successes, as well as areas for growth where you need support in meeting your planned desired results. Explicitly try to see your curricula through varied eyes and perspectives to enhance what you have already been teaching for years.

How to Implement the Strategy at Varied Grade Levels

Elementary	Middle	High
Consider your desired results through the lens of students newer to academics and their continued personal and social development. When planning, ask yourself: *What knowledge, skills, and dispositions do students need to be successful in my classroom? *Which interpersonal and intrapersonal skills can I support alongside this academic learning?	Consider your desired results through the lens of early adolescence and continued academic development. When planning, ask yourself: *How might my students benefit from the knowledge, skills, and dispositions that I am teaching as they navigate hormonal changes, shifts in social hierarchy, and possible changes in their family interactions? *In what ways do I want students to grapple with big ideas or challenge themselves?	Consider your desired results through the lens of students who have college and/or careers on the horizon. When planning, ask yourself: *What knowledge, skills, and dispositions will students need to be successful after graduation? *How might students add their voice in determining learning goals based on standards, past experience, or ways they know they want to develop?

GUIDING QUESTIONS

As you read through this chapter, consider the following:

1. Which desired results matter most to me and my students?
2. What have I learned about my students, and how am I applying that knowledge to my planning?
3. Which topics or issues matter most to my students?
4. Which skills do my students need to develop? How can I build on their strengths to help?
5. How can I help students recognize the ways that the knowledge, skills, and dispositions they are developing transfer to other classes and outside of school?

STRATEGY 6: DETERMINING LEARNING GOALS

> Teacher Contributors
> Lianne Jones, Westlake Preparatory Lutheran Academy (TX), 5th–8th grades
> Jean Wassel, Rex Putnam High School (OR), 10th–12th grades

Determining learning goals is about deciding the big ideas, skills, and dispositions you want your students to develop so that a clear plan can be created. Having a clear end enables you to break down knowledge, skills, and dispositions (K/S/D) into manageable parts. This helps students understand how and why they are engaging in learning and sets a path for them to reach the end goals. By focusing on determining learning goals, teachers can implement the backward design process that ensures distinct alignment among the unit and lesson goals, assessments, and instructional practices.

Strategy Implementation

1. **Examine possible learning objectives.** After determining your unit or lesson topic, explore a wide range of learning standards or objectives related to the topic. Objectives can be based on:
   - *State/District/School Curriculum Objectives:* Gather all the mandated curricular objectives that your school is required to use, including if you teach Advanced Placement or International Baccalaureate courses, and read over each objective to understand the different elements of the unit you are required to teach. If your district does not have mandated or suggested standards and objectives, look to larger school districts that post their standards and objectives on their websites.
     - As you read the objectives, make notes of key ideas and concepts that they are trying to achieve.
     - Determine if there are any ideas and concepts that are missing from the mandated curriculum, and add them to the list of objectives.
     - NOTE: If you are teaching an elective course or one that is not aligned with standard curriculum, brainstorm possible objectives that relate to your unit topic. Create a list of objectives without worrying about how they are organized or sequenced.
   - *Knowledge/Skills/Dispositions:* Ensure you are accounting for possible K/S/D that students are expected to learn over the course of your unit. This can help you decide whether your end goals are based on K/S/D or some combination of the three. It can be helpful to pay attention to the verbs in the objectives when considering skills and dispositions. The actions that students are taking (e.g., analyze and collaborate) are often strong indicators of the skills and dispositions involved in their learning.

2. **Chunk learning objectives.** After gathering all the possible objectives for your unit, sort them by themes to help determine overarching ideas and goals that emerge. Different types of themes to consider include:
   - *Content-Specific:* Group all of the content-based objectives and create subgroups to determine themes that exist across the content. Then determine if there are one or two overarching themes that emerge and frame all the content well.
   - *Connection to Self/Society:* Look at all the content-specific themes, and list any ways they might connect to society or students' lives.
   - *Action/Application:* Chunk any objectives that focus on action or practical application of the content students are learning.
   - *Skills/Dispositions:* Find any objectives that relate to skills and dispositions and complement how and why the content will be taught.

Make Your Goals Applicable to the Real World

Always ensure that the end goal has application to the real world. Constantly try to get students to think bigger about where content is useful and applicable. "Why is this relevant to me and where can I see this in my life?" Making real world applications creates buy-in; they need to "see the point" and it will motivate them to do it. If they understand why they are learning something they are more likely to engage in the process.

—Lianne Jones

---

3. **Determine the overarching/end goal(s).** Even if your mandated curriculum provides overarching goals, ensure that the way those goals are framed reflects the intended goals for your classroom and students. (It is most important that the goals work best for your students, even if they stray from mandated goals slightly.) These goals can be content-specific, connection to self or society, action or application, or skills or dispositions. It can be useful to limit the number of overarching goals to a maximum of three so the unit retains focus and does not feel like a compilation of parts without a clearly defined goal and end result.

4. **Consider how students will perform to meet end goals.** After drafting your end goals, think about how well your students will be able to meet those goals. Consider goals that are SMART, that is, specific, measurable, achievable, relevant, and timely (Doran, 1981). If you determine that the goals do not meet that criteria, adjust them so they do.

5. **Plan your assessments and instructional practices.** Plan your summative and formative assessments and instructional practices with your end goals in mind. Consider the pacing and flow of the unit to ensure the instructional practices prepare students for success in meeting the goals and that the assessments reflect progress toward the goals.

6. **Revisit the end goal(s).** Evaluate your assessments and instructional practices to determine whether they are in direct alignment with your end goals. If they are not, adjust your end goals to match the assessments and instructional practices, or adjust your assessments or instructional practices to better fit your end goals.

7. **Test out and adapt the end goals as needed.** Work through the process you have created for your students to evaluate whether you can achieve your end goals using the steps and supports you set up (e.g., if you want your students in a math class to work out problems without a calculator, do it yourself to see what obstacles your students will encounter so you can better prepare them; this will help you adapt your goals and processes as needed). If you determine you are having difficulty achieving the end goals, decide whether you need to adjust the end goals or your plan of action to meet those goals.

8. **Confer with colleagues.** Either during the planning process or after you have come up with your end goals, share your end goals with colleagues inside or outside of your content area to ensure they effectively encapsulate the key concepts of your unit and are clear for any of your students to understand and achieve.

STRATEGY IN ACTION: COLLABORATING TO DETERMINE LEARNING GOALS

In my first few years teaching, I worked with a collaborative team that utilized this strategy. At the beginning of each grading term, we would use district-provided unit plans to identify the main learning components and "pencil them in" on our calendar days. We would also add school functions, holidays, and so on in our planning. This provided a framework from which to plan lessons in detail as the weeks progressed. This process also helped ensure that we were teaching everything we were supposed to!

Sometimes the district would provide essential questions. Those questions served as our guiding posts as we were thinking about the details of each day. We constructed a sequence toward meeting our end goals and aligned each objective with the essential question(s). If given a weaker essential question, we would look at the objectives and try to figure out the relevance for them and then create our own essential questions that tied different things together and/or connected to the real world. This would serve as our constant benchmark. Is our planning and sequence aligning with that question?

As a new teacher, this process was invaluable to my development and provided a systematic way of roadmapping instruction. Later in my career, I was the sole middle school math teacher for 5th- to 8th-grade students and was tasked with creating similar calendars for four levels of mathematics. This strategy was critical in my organization and weekly lesson planning!

—*Lianne Jones*

9. **Write your end goals and make them visible.** Always write your end goals in student-friendly language that is accessible to all your students. It is also useful to create visuals or anchor charts of where the unit is going (your end goals) and steps along the way to meet those goals. Having your end goals and the process visible for your students will help the class understand where they are throughout the unit in their progression toward achieving the end goals.

Going beyond the Superficial

I need to make sure my students are learning the concepts on more than a superficial level. The students need to learn in a strategic enough way that it sticks. Students are used to learning at a more superficial level and they are going through the motions waiting to be helped out. The biggest part of backwards planning is knowing what the end is because it allows students the ability to chunk and retain information for longer-term learning of concepts.

—Jean Wassel

WHY I LIKE THIS STRATEGY

You run out of time if you don't plan ahead; planning ahead really helps with pacing! Knowing in general how much time you have and need helps you plan more thoughtfully . . . when you're more thoughtful about things you're able to get things done and it saves time.

—Lianne Jones

As a support teacher, you're focusing on what's most urgent at the time. That relies on students advocating for themselves and makes it easier for students to hide. It's not strategic to just put out fires in front of you. When there's more of a plan, you can organize things—with the end in mind—you can build in support for students more proactively.

—Jean Wassel

Adaptation for Different Assets and Needs

Planning Time	
Limited Time	*Lots of Time*
*Start with the big ideas, and then figure out the order and sequencing of the unit.	*Focus on collaborating with colleagues and adapting your end goals and plans based on what has worked for them and what is best for your students.
*Fill in all of the other gaps as you go.	
	*Revisit your end goals and plans throughout the unit, adapting as needed, and then reflect on those plans and goals after the unit concludes.

Opportunity to Collaborate	
Limited Opportunity	*Lots of Opportunity*
*Reach out to teachers at other schools or teacher communities online.out to teachers at other schools or online communities of teachers.	*Engage in "planning rounds" similar to "instructional rounds" where teachers can take turns workshopping ideas for their planning.
*Create a working group of teachers in different content areas to workshop and support one another in the planning process.	*Find multiple spaces to collaborate from within your school to across your district and beyond. Compare and contrast how different teachers are planning similar content to meet the needs of their students, and then adapt to meet the needs of yours.

> **STRATEGY IN ACTION: PLANNING AS A SPECIAL EDUCATION CO-TEACHER OR SUPPORT TEACHER**
>
> I began informally focusing on determining learning goals last year when I co-taught a math support class with a general education International Baccalaureate (IB) Math teacher. We were working with juniors in IB Math Applications. Students at our school have a block schedule with four periods per day; one of their eight periods was their general ed IB Math class. Another period was spent in our math support class.
>
> I used to plan more reactively rather than thinking proactively about what and how to plan. You can have a plan and then something changes; the ability to be flexible and get to know your students and change your instruction based on your students and do things based on who your students are. You just need to balance getting to know your students, planning ahead, and having a longer-term plan in mind.
>
> Planning with the end in mind helps to organize larger, overarching goals, and as a support teacher, teaching so many different things at once, this is critical. Having structure to it and an end goal in mind helps to both create and follow through with the plan. That's what was really helpful in my co-teaching because as students moved to IB classes without the prerequisite skills, it required more proactive planning than reactive. Planning this way helped me to better understand how to support the teaching of prerequisite skills.
>
> —*Jean Wassel*

STRATEGY 7: THEMATIC PLANNING

> Teacher Contributors
> *Kristin DeLorenzo, Francis A. Desmares Elementary School (NJ), 1st–4th grades*
> *Emily Workman, EdD, Brentwood High School (TN), 9th grade*

Thematic planning centers on lessons and units of study around a particular idea to provide a strong rationale for learning. The themes that you choose can help with engagement and interdisciplinary learning and support student connection between their present learning and their future endeavors.

Strategy Implementation

1. **Choose themes.** Even if your curriculum is already established, you can organize what you teach according to theme. Consider the *why* behind student learning, and focus on big ideas and important skills. Ask yourself why the curriculum matters to your students, and emphasize those reasons as you plan. You can choose a theme for the school year or marking period that unites each unit, and then consider how specific units support those larger themes.
   - *Determine Big Themes for the Year or Marking Period:* Before the school year starts, take time to uncover optimal themes for your course. To do this:
     - *Review Material/Units:* Look for commonalities and connection in materials/units for the year. Remember, themes may relate to content, skills, and/or dispositions. Examples include:
       - *English:* Power and difficult choices
       - *Math:* Perseverance and attention to detail
       - *Social Studies:* Learning from our past and influencing our future
       - *Science:* Cause and effect
       - *Art/Music:* Finding your style
     - *Connect with Current Events:* When coming up with themes, consider what events are going on locally, nationally, and globally. This will help you design and create themes that are meaningful and relevant to the students. For instance, if it is an election year, you might focus on voice and impact. If your town or school is having an anniversary, consider focusing on important elements of that history.
     - *Act Local/Think Global:* Come up with themes that are relevant to your students, but also connect with the larger global community. For example, consider local people who have made a big difference in your world. Connect their actions with your curriculum and look for global parallels to their work.

> When we follow a series of lessons day-to-day, it is easy to get bogged down in what we are doing each day rather than taking a broad view and showing how the lessons are connected.
>
> —Emily Workman

- *Choose Unit Themes:* Once you figure out your larger themes for the year, consider how individual units can fit thematically into the larger course themes. Also think about which student interests, strengths, and areas of growth to focus on within each unit:
    - *Connect with Yearlong and/or Marking Period Themes:* Ask yourself how each unit fits into the larger course theme(s), and then identify elements from each unit that can serve as subthemes of the larger course themes. When establishing each unit theme, ensure that the unit themes build on one another toward the end goal(s) of the course (see *Strategy 6: Determining Learning Goals*), which will help students connect with past and future learning (see *Strategy 9: Connecting with Previous Learning*).

Know the Big Picture

Sometimes we think that we are teaching a concept/skill, but students can often just be repeating a process by rote. If we have a big picture of what students have been learning, we can reach back and remind students of the learning they've had and help them see they are doing something that extends from what they were doing.

—Kristin DeLorenzo

- *Focus on Areas for Students' Interests, Strengths, and Areas for Growth:* When identifying unit themes, look beyond the content and take into consideration students' interests, strengths, and areas for growth to help students authentically connect with their learning. Consider:
    - *Interests:* If students are interested in Pokémon, look for ways to connect their learning through a Pokémon theme. (See *Strategy 17: Connecting Skills and Content with Students' Lives and Interests*.)
    - *Strengths:* If students are great at complaining, design a unit that turns problems into complaints, and have students focus on how to respond.
    - *Areas for Growth:* If students need to work on summarizing, incorporate summarizing into most lessons in your unit, and develop a guideline for assessing progress (see *Strategy 11: Creating Effective Rubrics*).
- *Consider Timing:* Think about how this unit aligns with events that may be happening in your local area, national or local holidays that relate to your unit, or if you might want to be outdoors or observe something seasonal in relation to the unit. Examples include:
    - *Local Events:* If your town has an annual pancake breakfast for the local fire department, you may want to focus on local heroes during that month.
    - *National Holidays:* April is National Poetry Month. This is a great time to dive into reading poetry together as a class.
    - *Weather:* If you are studying Monarch butterflies, look into their migratory pattern and when it would make sense to raise them and set them free to migrate.

> By taking a higher-level, thematic unit perspective, I feel more freedom in the day-to-day teaching of mathematics. It becomes less about the lessons "in the book" and more about the standards. This gives me the freedom to choose the best tasks and resources for my students at any given time.
>
> —*Kristin DeLorenzo*

2. **Connect themes across disciplines.** Think broadly when it comes to determining themes that connect content areas.
   - *Talk It out with Your Colleagues:* Look for natural connections, and be willing to change the order of your units to better align what you are teaching with your colleagues' calendars. For instance:
     - If students are writing a persuasive paragraph for their health class, consider focusing on persuasive writing in English or social studies at the same time. When aligning your units, discuss social skills or dispositions that you'd like to see students developing, and work together to determine how each of your content areas can relate.
     - If you are an elementary school teacher developing units in various content areas, have these conversations with your grade-level colleagues, and work together to determine connections.
   - *Connect Themes Based on Content, Skills, and/or Dispositions:* There are multiple ways to connect your course themes with multiple disciplines. Consider the following examples for content-, skill-, and disposition-based themes:
     - *Content-Based Themes:* If you are focusing on the theme of power in English, find out how this could connect with other content areas. Social studies is a natural fit with rulers, war, and social status, but you can branch out further. For instance, look at power in science. Could this relate to the food chain or to environmental impacts of choices by people in power?
     - *Skills-Based Themes:* If students are learning to find the lowest common denominator in math, encourage them to look for commonalities in reading, science, and social studies. This can even extend to social emotional learning. Look for commonalities among people in your class (e.g., liking music or sports, enjoying working together, staying organized). How do these commonalities help students connect with each other and work effectively?
     - *Dispositions-Based Themes:* Sometimes themes are based on personal traits students want students to develop. Across all disciplines you might connect students' experiences based on dispositions such as perseverance, collaboration, taking initiative, and curiosity.

3. **Ensure a safe space for exploring themes.** Learning and growing together can be challenging. Work to create a space where students know their voices will be heard, questioning is encouraged, and mistakes are a part of the learning process. To do this:
   - *Spotlight Student Voice:* To elevate students' voices most effectively and safely, consider:

- *Asking Students about What Matters to Them:* Start the year with a survey about students' interests and passions (see *Strategy 17: Connecting Skills and Content with Students' Lives and Interest* for more ideas). Look for ways to connect students' responses to the themes you've selected.
- *Going "Off Course":* Even if you don't have time to develop an entirely new unit based on students' interest, you should have time to take a day to explore something that clearly excites students or to embed that topic into an existing unit.
- *Following up on Divergent Viewpoints:* If students see a topic from a different point of view than what is presented, be sure to make time to ask them to share more about their understanding or to ask questions that delve into this further. And if students all share the same viewpoint, think about infusing diverse perspectives they might not have considered.

- *Encourage Questioning:* Create an environment in which students feel empowered to ask questions. To help student with this:
  - *Model Questioning:* If students know that you need to ask questions to learn more, they are more likely to do this too.
  - *Provide Opportunity:* Give students a chance to pose questions based on what they notice or wonder about a topic. This type of questioning is low stakes and sets the stage for continued questioning throughout the unit.
  - *Use Question Structures*: Consider the types of questions that you or your students may need to ask and create stems, such as:
    - *Initial Questions:*
      - What is this unit about?
      - Why is this topic or skill important to me?
      - What knowledge and skills do I need to be successful?
    - *Clarifying Questions:*
      - I think you said _____. Is that correct?
      - Do you mean _____?
    - *Follow-Up Questions:*
      - Will you tell me more about ____?
      - If _____, then _____?
    - *Probing Questions:*
      - Why do you think _____?
      - Have you considered _____?

> My place is not to pass judgment. My place is to give kids a safe place to land.
>
> —Emily Workman

> Sometimes learning isn't about being groundbreaking; it's about breaking it down. Asking good questions helps us to do that!
>
> —Kristin DeLorenzo

- *Be Willing to Fail:* Mistakes are part of the process. Therefore:
  - Share your own mistakes and how you learned from them.
  - Share mistakes made by famous people who students consider smart or successful.
  - Model how mistakes help us know where we need to grow. Focus on knowledge and skills development that becomes apparent based on mistakes during the learning process.

> Learning is not about expecting perfection. If we fall short, that's where our greatest learning opportunities lie.
>
> —Emily Workman

STRATEGY IN ACTION: KEY MATHEMATICAL UNDERSTANDINGS

A few years ago, I had a new teaching assignment which required that I co-teach grade 5 mathematics in a classroom with a very diverse set of learners. As my co-teacher, Dan and I began planning a unit on place value and multiplication, we realized quickly that we needed to be on the same page as to what we wanted students to learn and how we were going to deliver the material.

This was new learning for some of the students. We knew what the tests asked for, but we wanted to go further. So often in teaching about multiplication of decimals, students just learn the process of moving the decimal. We wanted them to understand that this is a place value shift. With this in mind, we focused our language and our teaching around place values and what moving that decimal means. Rather than teaching a rule, we taught the concept behind the rule.

Our most productive planning occurred when we asked ourselves, "How will we know that students have mastered this topic?" For us, it was much more than the grade on the unit assessment. In fact, that final assessment was almost irrelevant, because our careful planning had given us the tools to assess along the way. We paid careful attention to language and how students talked about what they were doing. Because of this, we already knew how students would perform on the test before we gave it.

Throughout the unit, it was so powerful to sit and listen to students talk about their process. When they were using language like "place value shift" rather than saying "I'm moving the decimal," we knew that they were learning the concept in a deeper way.

When I switched roles and moved into teaching elementary gifted and talented mathematics, I naturally planned using backward design. My first year of this role was during the pandemic, and it was essential that I identify the big ideas and help students make connections because we simply did not have enough time to teach all of the content. Using Understanding by Design® (Wiggins & McTighe, 2005) helped me to focus on the most important ideas of the unit. Since I was also learning fourth grade content, focusing on the big ideas and end of unit student outcomes helped me to understand the new standards.

—Kristin DeLorenzo

> ## WHY I LIKE THIS STRATEGY
>
> Thematic planning looks at the curriculum as a whole unit rather than pieces of standards. By utilizing an overarching theme, I can bridge different pieces of literature (or other curriculum) in a way that provides real world connections that will enable students to deepen their understanding of the content.
>
> *—Emily Workman*
>
> Mathematics is a beautifully connected subject, but can often feel disconnected when taught from a teacher's manual with a day-to-day perspective. It is easy to lose sight of the big ideas and natural connections when the focus is on practicing skills in workbooks. Thematic planning keeps me focused on helping students to see how the math is connected within the grade level, and also connected to what they already have learned.
>
> *—Kristin DeLorenzo*

Adaptation for Different Assets and Needs

Curriculum

Mandated Curriculum

*Find important and relatable themes within your mandated curriculum.

*Think outside the box about the material that you must teach and how it can be connected to more relatable themes if needed. Make these connections while still keeping clear about how you are adhering to the required elements of the curriculum.

Curricular Freedom

*Be bold. Design themes that are clear and meaningful to your students. Find texts and resources that align with these themes and are explicitly connected to the students' lives and interests.

*Get student input. Ask students what they want to read or what skills they want to develop. Likely what they share can be incorporated into your plans while still supporting advancement toward thematic learning goals. In fact, they may give you feedback that leads them beyond goals that you selected.

Academic Diversity

Limited Diversity

*Consider frontloading information, and then giving students a chance to explore a topic or show their ability with a skill in their own way.

*Look for opportunities for students to show ways that their thinking differs from others. This will keep the class student-centered rather than topic-centered or teacher-centered.

Lots of Diversity

*Have a challenge question ready to go for learners who are making connections quickly.

*For students who are struggling, be ready to support their understanding of themes and their ability to connect their work with the big ideas, skills, and dispositions you are highlighting. Be open to alternate ways of showing success (See *Strategy 13: Student Choice in How to Represent Learning*).

STRATEGY IN ACTION: INTERDISCIPLINARY THEMES

Early in my career I taught at a private middle school. Because the school was very small, I was the only eighth-grade ELA teacher and we really worked quite autonomously, which kept me from developing the skill set I needed to think about how my content worked with other courses.

It wasn't until I moved to a bigger high school that I finally had my own "light bulb moment" when it came to cross-curriculum planning. As I was sitting in a grade-level faculty meeting, one of the science teachers was lamenting how she was struggling with strategies to teach persuasive language in her nutrition class. This is the moment when it all finally clicked. In my class, we were moving into the unit covering ethos, logos, and pathos. Using the Declaration of Independence as my anchor literature work, the plan was to dive into Thomas Jefferson's words to analyze his rhetoric and verbiage to move the colonists to the side of creating a new America.

After talking with the nutrition teacher, I began brainstorming ways in which I could make connections to her content in my class. One evening, I was watching television with my family and a breakfast cereal commercial came on the screen. In that moment it hit me: I could make my ethos-logos-pathos connection to nutrition through cereal. In my class, my students worked in groups to create their own cereal. They had to determine their audience, create a skeleton marketing campaign, and create a poster of a mockup of their cereal box. (These were hung in the hallway for a while.) Students then presented their cereal to the class with a piece of their presentation focusing on how they used ethos, logos, and pathos in their marketing.

Moving to the nutrition class, the teacher was able to build on the foundation I set in my class to transfer the knowledge to the idea of informative presentations about food choices, diets, exercise, and so on. While not all of her students were enrolled in my classes, the students we had in common were able to work with their classmates to share the information. Thus, her student presentations were more thoughtful and were grounded more in rhetorical devices than before.

The lesson I learned when I came to planning cross-curriculum is that I did not have to completely throw out what I was doing to work with another content area. The beauty comes in when you are able to blend the two subject areas: The students are able to see how the subjects they are learning about can be applied to other areas, hence, making my content richer and more valuable to their lives.

—*Emily Workman*

STRATEGY 8: CONNECTING STUDENTS WITH LEARNING GOALS

> Teacher Contributors
> *Kathleen Stigliano, Pond Road Elementary School (NJ), PreK–4th grades*
> *Chris Saunders, Brentwood High School (TN), 9th grade*

When you plan, you are planning for your current students and not your former students or your ideal students. Make learning engaging and meaningful by considering how best to connect curriculum with students' interests, how to support students as they are learning, and ways to extend learning and opportunities for choice.

Strategy Implementation

Part I: Use What You Learn about Your Students

1. **Use what students share.** You can learn about your students *directly* by engaging in conversation and get-to-know-you activities and *indirectly* through surveys and conversations with other teachers who have worked with your students. Adapt your planning based on:
   - *Interests:* Common areas of interest that you can incorporate into planning include: sports, TV shows or movies, gaming, animals, the environment, social justice, and so on.
   - *Learning Preferences:* Find out *how* students prefer to learn: visual, auditory, kinesthetic, independent, group work, teacher-directed, or student-directed. Add students' preferred learning methods to your planning, and challenge students to try new ways of learning.
   - *Prior Learning that Has "Stuck":* Remember that just because something has been taught doesn't mean that the learning has stuck. Ask students what they remember about topics or experiences related to your curriculum. Build from the concepts and skills that seem solid.
   - *Values and Culture:* Think about what may be important to students based on their values and culture both within school and outside of school. (See *Strategy 5: Culturally Responsive/Sustaining Teaching*). Consider what matters to students in terms of:
     - *Current Social Capital:* fashion, sports, music, art.
     - *Morals/Family Values:* religion, rituals, family time together, honesty, hard work.
     - *Their Future as Learners/Members of Society:* getting a job, helping others, making a positive impact on their community.

> Take time at the beginning of the school year to learn about students. Who are they as learners? Are they a learner who you think isn't paying attention but winds up taking it all in? Are they a learner who needs active engagement? What are their interests outside of school? How can you incorporate this into planning and instruction?
>
> —*Kathleen Stigliano*

2. **Connect with other teachers.** Colleagues who currently teach your students or who taught your students in the past can provide perspectives that students may not choose to share or that students don't note for themselves. When talking to your colleagues:
   - *Understand the Learner:* Learn more about students by asking colleagues:
     ◦ Where they saw students shine as learners.
     ◦ Areas of struggle with understanding or skills development.
     ◦ Strong beliefs that students hold.
     ◦ Possible misconceptions that students may carry.
   - *Adapt Planning/Instruction:* Engage in discussions about planning and teaching by asking colleagues:
     ◦ How they adapted content to match with students' interest.
     ◦ Impactful supports they provided for struggling students.
     ◦ Ways they challenged or extended learning for students who were excelling.

Part II: Plan with Students in Mind

1. **Make objectives clear to students.** Your learners need to know *why* they are doing what they are doing. Plan with objectives in mind and the intention of making sure that students understand the objectives. To do this:
   - *Know Your Rationale:* Be prepared to explain the *why* behind each unit and lesson.
   - *Keep Your Objectives in Mind:* Use your objectives to help you decide what to include and what to cut from each unit/lesson. This will ultimately streamline your planning time and help you make decisions more efficiently.
   - *Check for Understanding:* Ask students if they understand the objectives behind their learning. If their answer is "yes," then great! If their answer is "no," then consider how to make your objectives and the connections between your objectives and their work clearer. You may:
     ◦ Post unit objectives and refer to them regularly.
     ◦ Post lesson objectives at the start of each day and ask how students met those objectives at the end of each lesson.
     ◦ Get yourself and students in the habit of pausing during a lesson to reflect on how they are meeting their objectives and any areas of confusion they need to address. This will likely influence future plans.

2. **Think about inclusive and meaningful content.** It's important to think about content based on student interest and how students may respond. A topic that is interesting to one student may be controversial or boring to another. (For more on this, see *Strategy 17: Connecting Skills and Content to Students' Lives and Interests*.) To help you plan, consider:
   - *Content that Appeals to Most of the Class:* Look for small tweaks to your curriculum that you can make to situate student learning in a topic that matters to most students. For example, if most students in your class are into sneakers, and the topic you are teaching is percentages, focus on the increase in value of a pair of sneakers if kept pristine after purchasing.

- *Ways to Vary How You Situate Learning*: Be sure to bring in a range of topics so you can hook each of your learners at different points. For example, if you use a sports theme for several lessons, switch things up, and move to an animal or superhero theme.

The Value of Check-Ins for Planning

It's important to have periodic check-ins throughout the year because we know students change so much. See what they are still into and what is new. It's great to do this during morning meetings, conferences, or before/after lunch or specials. It can be a great brain break that has a lot of value for planning.

—*Kathleen Stigliano*

- *Consider Students' Comfort or Alternative Views:* To account for your students' comfort with content while also infusing alternative views, look at your resources and materials and ask yourself:
  ◦ Which voices are represented?
  ◦ Which voices are missing?
  ◦ How will students see themselves and others when learning this content?
  ◦ Are varied viewpoints represented?
  ◦ What knowledge and beliefs do students bring to the topic? To answer this:
    - Acknowledge students' schema and values.
    - Communicate the objectives so students see the *why* behind exploring the topic.
    - Discuss varied opinions or viewpoints in a safe and respectful manner.

3. **Vary process and product.** There are so many ways to vary process and product during the learning experience; however, it is important to remember the value of providing routines that support students developing habits of success. When planning, think about creating a good balance between the comfort of routine and the engagement that comes from choice and variation. To do this:
   - *Determine Routines:* Find routines that work for you and your students and make them integral parts of your plans. (For more information on "Routines," read our first book in the series, *Adaptable Teaching: 30 Practical Strategies for All School Contexts*.) Some routines that engage and motivate learners include:
     ◦ *Opening Routines:* Develop routines to open class that help students transition into the start of class. Consider:
       - *Grounding:* Allocate two minutes to settle into seats and take a collective breath as a class. You can also get the wiggles out by having students shake their arms and legs or by having a dance to start class.
       - *Check-In:* Plan time for daily check-ins with students. This may be a full-class question that all students answer in a few words or with a picture, or it can be something you do individually as students are working on an initial task.

- *Routines for Classwork:* After the start of class, you want to have routines related directly to the classwork students engage in throughout the class period. This includes:
  - *Note-Taking:* Give students opportunities to develop their own style of note-taking, such as:
    - Creating materials with semistructured outlines for students to complete.
    - Using graphic organizers.
    - Including higher-order questions or prompts within interactive slides, or other materials, so students use the information they are learning.
    - Having a system for organizing classwork in physical or electronic folders for each unit.
  - *Transitions to Group or Independent Work:* Develop a routine that works for you and your students. For example, each time you move to independent or group work, you may want to:
    - Review directions posted on the board.
    - Remind students that directions are also posted on materials.
    - If working in groups, have a predictable setup for where groups will meet and how they will arrange desks and chairs to show they are ready to work productively together.
    - Know how you will distribute materials. (Will you have materials collated and ready for one group member to pick up? Will they be at the table?)
    - Have a cleanup plan. Where do students put works-in-progress, completed work, supplies, and other materials?
  - *Test Review:* Help students feel prepared for tests or assessments by having predictable steps they can take:
    - Review objectives of the unit and students' learning experiences, and help students highlight key ideas or skills that will be part of the assessment.
    - Develop review games that engage students. Online platforms such as Kahoot or Gimkit can be useful for this.
  - *Presentations:* When students are giving presentations, develop routines for presenters and audience members. Because public speaking is anxiety-provoking for many students, having routines in place for this is especially important. Consider:
    - A location for the presenter (this could be a podium, a space by the door, or even a classroom stage).
    - How the presenter will know they have the audience's attention. Is there a call and response? Is it about eye contact?
    - Ways for the audience to respond to the presenter. For example, snaps for support, clapping at the end of the presentation, respectful questioning, thanking presenters for their work.
- *Routines for Closing the Day:* Use a physical paper exit ticket or an online survey asking students to:
  - Connect what they did during class with the lesson objectives.

- Rate confidence or understanding.
- Pose questions for future learning.
- Ask for what they need.
- *Provide Choice:* Offer choices for how students learn and show their growth. Possibilities include:
  - *Expose Students to Different Ways of Learning:* When you incorporate varied methods of learning into your plans, you give students the opportunity to determine methods that work best for them. When planning for whole or small group instruction, include video, audio, note-taking, graphic organizers, group work, individual work, and so on. Provide opportunities for students to discuss what approach worked well for them and why it worked.

> I think it's important for kids to learn how a group of people working together needs to include different roles. It doesn't have to be a group of like-minded individuals with similar interests and skills. We need variety!
>
> —*Kathleen Stigliano*

  - *Plan options for process and product:* Offer a choice board or checklist for success. (See *Strategy 13: Student Choice in How to Represent Learning.*) When planning student options, be sure the choices are all connected with the learning objectives.

4. **Support and extend learning.** When considering the learners in your classroom, think about how you both support and extend their learning to meet their needs.
   - *Support:* If you have concerns about student readiness for learning, you may need to adapt your plans to meet students where they are. This can mean having students work at a different pace from one another or work in different ways. Although this may seem daunting at first, you can support differentiation by:
     - *Developing Learning Agendas:* Share the goal for the day, and help students recognize the steps they need to take to achieve that goal. Create checkpoints along the way so you can see how students are progressing and provide support as needed.
     - *Providing Leveled Readings to Support Learning:* Use sites like Newsela.com to easily adapt the Lexile score on readings.
     - *Conferencing:* Allot time for conferencing with individuals and groups to determine what information or skills they need.
     - *Developing a Protocol:* Check in with groups and encourage participation from all group members. This may mean pulling quieter students aside or providing an encouraging word to students who haven't fully engaged.

- *Extend:* When you have students who are excelling at a unit, you may want to:
  - *Go Deeper:* Consider ways for students to dive deeper into an aspect of the unit that is meaningful to them.
  - *Become an Expert:* Provide students with an opportunity to be the resident expert. Let them know some components of the topic that students need to know about and invite them to take the lead on researching and presenting.

STRATEGY IN ACTION: CONNECTING LEARNERS AND GOALS APPLIES TO ADULTS TOO

Since moving from teaching in the classroom to my role as an administrator, I find myself continuing to approach my planning with my learners in mind when working with adult learners during workshops, data team meetings, faculty meetings, and so on. It is so important to make sure that faculty are engaged and working effectively, especially after a long day of teaching!

When we were reviewing and analyzing data, I wanted to be sure that faculty felt invested and ready to dive in. First, we identified our end goal. Why are we meeting? What exactly are we looking to accomplish today? By analyzing this data, what is our ultimate goal? How will our work today help students grow?

Next, we identified ways in which we could approach the data and how we could best organize ourselves. Is there a specific protocol that could be used that would help us accomplish our goal? Is a general, more open and free-structured discussion better? Should we chunk the data or look at it as a whole? How should we record our findings? Are we going to split up into groups or work independently?

Finally, we identified the specific areas of data that needed to be analyzed based on our goals. From there, we were able to isolate two different protocols. One was less structured, a fishbowl approach that involved discussing the data and observing/taking notes on the discussion. The second approach was more structured; teachers identified how many minutes they wanted to spend on each data set and key questions to keep in mind when reviewing. It was interesting to note that newer teachers preferred the second option because they felt more confident with clear timing and guided questions for support.

With both approaches, the end goals remained the same in terms of what we wanted to learn from the data. Determining process options together allowed us to be sure that all team members understood their options and the responsibilities of each team member. Taking the time to clearly articulate goals and to adapt the process to meet the needs of my learners enabled us to work efficiently and effectively. Adult learners need to be considered too!

—*Kathleen Stigliano*

WHY I LIKE THIS STRATEGY

I have learned a lot about providing different opportunities for different students. Not all students benefit from learning in the same way. Ultimately, the reality of teaching is that our strategies continue to evolve each year because we must adapt to students and alter plans based on the effectiveness of the previous year and based on who the learners are at the time.

—*Chris Saunders*

I use *Understanding by Design®* (Wiggins & McTighe, 2005) to structure my approach to considering my learners because the "big picture" helps me keep my learners and my end goal in focus. I differentiate and modify instruction and assignments more inherently, rather than taking a preexisting "traditional" plan and tweaking it. This approach also clearly defined the answer to "Why do I need to learn this?" from my more skeptical learners.

—*Kathleen Stigliano*

STRATEGY IN ACTION: TRIVIA TEST REVIEW

Before any major test, I give students the opportunity to assess their own learning, trivia-game style. This self-assessment followed by a full class pretest Kahoot lets me know what needs clarifying and where my students are solid in their learning.

First, I share review pages and corresponding slides paired with each component of the unit. Students have an allotted amount of time (displayed on the screen) to work in teams to complete various components of review. Sometimes I let students choose their teams; sometimes, I choose students for teams randomly; and sometimes, I seemingly choose randomly, but I really have ideal teams in mind as I count off. I typically choose groups based on how well students will work together rather than high/low academic performance.

During team-based trivia, students review geography, identify terms, and explain events in detail. Students then ask questions from their unit study guide, and we discuss the answers as a whole class. I go over each component and address any questions that students cannot answer for each other.

Then it is time for students to compete individually. I use a Kahoot review game so I can see the data regarding which elements students need to better understand and which elements are "sticking."

Most of my students like this approach because they enjoy competing in groups and individually. Students who are not as competitive as others appreciate the group support before engaging individually. Offering a variety of review games gives students the opportunity to work with other classmates that may be higher or lower academically. I think this is very beneficial because students can teach or learn from one another. This is a fun way for me to interact with the class and offer whole-class and individual feedback.

—*Chris Saunders*

Adaptation for Different Assets and Needs

Technology	
Low Tech *Help students understand that they are more likely to focus on specifics related to a learning goals when they physically write down information using pen and paper as compared with typing on a device because they are more selective about what they write down. *Create low-tech shared documents by assigning students different ink colors so their individual work can be recognized, and you can have a sense of each student's interest and growth in relation to the learning goals.	***High Tech*** *Create Google Questions or Google Forms so you can analyze student understanding of and progress toward goals efficiently; adapt plans accordingly. *Use review tools like Kahoot and Blooket to get a sense of individual student learning in relation to the learning goals and to have some fun while doing so.

Cultural Diversity	
Limited Diversity *Take virtual field trips. Learn about a topic or place related to your content so students can develop new perspectives in relation to the lesson's learning goals. *Add activities that evaluate the *why* behind what students are learning, and provide opportunities for students to consider how this might matter beyond their own experiences. For example, analyze how learning about nutrition looks different, or matters in different ways, to students who live in areas that may have different access to food choices.	***Lots of Diversity*** *Create and support a culture of acceptance. (See *Strategy 5: Culturally Responsive/Sustaining Teaching.*) *Create an environment in which differences are valued and students are eager to learn about each other's cultures and experiences. Consider inviting family members or members of the community to come in to visit or present in relation to what you are learning. (See *Strategy 19: Considering Equity and Multiple Perspectives.*)

STRATEGY 9: CONNECTING WITH PREVIOUS LEARNING

> Teacher Contributors
> *James Connolly, AP Willits Elementary School (NY), Kindergarten–5th grades*
> *Eleanor Tixier, FDR Lima (Peru), 7th grade*

Students become successful when they can recognize connections between a topic and skills they are learning. When students build on their existing schema of knowledge and skills, they are likely to be more confident and competent as learners. When planning, look for ways to connect with prior learning, and include approaches that encourage students to keep track of their learning so they can apply it in the future.

Strategy Implementation

Part I: Finding out What Students Know

1. **Examine related and past curriculum.** Look at topics explored and skills used in your class, other content areas, and in prior grade levels. Consider ways to connect what students have learned with what you are planning to teach. For example:
   - *Content:* If students are discussing climate change in social studies, connect this with what they learned about different types of biospheres in a previous science unit.
   - *Skills:* If students are going to be writing research papers in English, connect this with the analysis and synthesis strategies they used when examining and talking about famous paintings in art class.
   - *Disposition:* If students are struggling to make progress, connect this with previous class conversations about growth mindset and perseverance.

2. **Ask students what they bring.** Remember, there is a difference between what you taught and what students learned. To get a better sense of what they actually learned, know, and believe:
   - *Pre-assess Learning:* At the start of any new unit, engage students in considering what they know about a topic already. You can do this with:
     - Full-class or individual brainstorming
     - Pretests
     - Class surveys
   - *Beliefs:* It is important to focus on what students believe about a topic. Therefore, pose unit-related questions to get a sense of student beliefs through:
     - Class discussions
     - Surveys
     - A physical Likert scale activity where students stand at different places according to the strength of their agreement or disagreement with a statement

- *Skills and Dispositions:* Either at the start of a unit or before a project gets underway, plan ways for students to think about the skills and dispositions they believe will be important to their success. To do this:
  - Review assignments together with a focus on skills and dispositions.
  - Provide time for students to think about what they already can do that will help them with the unit or project and where they want to grow.

3. **Make connections overt.** Think about ways to make the connections to previous learning clear for students. Examples include:
   - *Curriculum Map:* Create a visual curriculum map for display in the classroom so students can see the progression of their learning.
   - *Track Skills and Dispositions:* Keep track of skills and dispositions that students are developing on a bulletin board or an electronic platform. Refer to these skills often, so students get in the habit of making these connections.

Part II: Helping Students Connect Their Learning

1. **Most important point (MIP).** At the end of each lesson, plan to have students write down the most important point of the day. An ongoing list of MIPs will help students see how their learning connects with prior lessons; it will help you to know what big ideas or skills you need to plan to reinforce or expand on in future lessons; and at the end of the unit, students will have a comprehensive list of everything they learned.
   - *MIP Page:* Have students create an MIP page or make one for them. A page that you create may seem more formal at first. Students may feel more ownership if they create the pages themselves.
     - *Different Languages Are OK:* Even if students agree on the MIP, they do not need to all use the same language to write it on their page. Encourage students to record the MIP in their own words, so it makes sense to them.
     - *Not Agreeing Is OK:* Sometimes students will not agree on the MIP, which is fine. Students bring different schema, interests, and skills to each lesson, so their view of the MIP is likely to differ. If, for a particular lesson, you have determined that the MIP is non-negotiable, then you can make this clear.
   - *Make It Routine:* Integrate MIP pages into your daily plans. An optimal time to have students complete the MIP page is at the end of each class period as the closing activity. To stay organized and use time efficiently, either:
     - *Students Keep It:* Designate a space in students' notebooks, folders, or electronic documents where the page can easily be accessed.
     - *Collect It:* Collect the MIP pages each day so students' ideas don't get lost and so the routine of this reflection is clearly initiated by handing out the pages.
   - *Scaffold the Process:* Plan to ask students, "If someone were to ask you, what did you learn today in class, what would you put down?" Some student may benefit from scaffolding like the following:
     - What does the lesson title or objective tell you?
     - What did I have you underline?

- What did you write down?
- What skills did you use today?
- How could you synthesize this and write it in one sentence?

> I tell my students, "It's your page. If you want to write down two MIPs, that is OK. If it doesn't match your neighbor, that is OK." This is about students having ownership over their learning and keeping track of what they think is important.
>
> —*Eleanor Tixier*

- *Get Used to Reflecting:* As students get used to reflecting on the MIP, you can vary the process. Options for doing this include:
  - Rather than discussing as a full class, students can discuss with partners or in small groups.
  - Extend the MIP page to include two columns: *What I Learned* and *How I Learned* it.
  - Make time to discuss and make overt the connections between what students learned and what they are doing next.
- *MIPs as Assessment Prep:* Use the MIP page when preparing for summative assessments. To do this:
  - Review the MIP page as a class and discuss what will likely be included in a unit assessment.
  - Cross-reference the skills and knowledge on the MIP page with the rubric for a written or creative assignment related to the unit. The components should clearly align.

> The beauty of this is that it is easy, quick, cheap, simple, and it is something that everybody needs to be doing!
>
> —*Eleanor Tixier*

2. **Toolkits.** To help students recognize the ways that their learning transfers and to guide them in thinking about skills and knowledge that they want to develop, you can integrate toolkits into your planning. These toolkits support students in developing knowledge and applying learning strategies and problem-solving techniques to their academic pursuits.
   - *Design the Problem-Solving Toolkit:* Develop a way to introduce students to the Problem-Solving Toolkit, and communicate that they will use this continuously throughout the school year to help facilitate their learning and independence. To help with this:
     - *Create Examples:* Come up with examples of tools that students might want to include:
       - Growth mindset
       - Peer feedback
       - Spaced practice
       - Productive struggle

- Revising
- Retrieval practice
 ◦ *Design a Template:* Create a template that you can use to model possible components of a toolkit, including:
  - Tool description(s)
  - When you used it
  - How it helped
  - Ideas for using in the future

Should You Use Exemplars?

If you're going to use exemplars, you need to use very diverse exemplars so the options for formatting and topics remain open. Some 5th grade teachers chose not to show models to students and instead shared rubrics and "cherry-picked" elements of exemplary work such as helpful images or links to websites or brief videos that explain the chosen topic/skill.

—James Connolly

- *Develop Options for Toolkit Format and Organization:* Toolkits may be all digital or in physical notebooks. Therefore, break down how your students might use each option:
  ◦ *Digital:* With digital toolkits, set it up where students can include hyperlinks and a table of contents with a home button for easy navigation.
  ◦ *Physical:* With physical toolkits, design it where students can choose to use sticky notes to label tabs for sections.
- *Organize:* Students may want to organize by content area, type of skill (writing, listening, persevering), or theme. Set up the toolkit with options for how students can organize in a way that works for them.
- *Reflect:* Set a time for students to reflect. Work this into your daily routine intentionally. Also, look for moments on the spot that are ripe for reflection and recording in the toolkit. Possible toolkit times include:
  ◦ Before transitioning to a new subject.
  ◦ After lunch or a "special" to help students refocus.

An Example of Transfer from Math to Social Emotional Learning

We started the year with fractions and worked with the theme, *Finding Common Ground*. In addition to paying attention to resources (skill overview pages, videos) that helped students conceptualize how to make common decimals and common fractions, teachers and students focused on social emotional learning (SEL) tools that helped them find common ground with one another and form friendships or provide support during productive struggle. This was challenging for many students, and thus showed the importance of taking time to focus on the SEL component.

—James Connolly

- When things are "clicking" and students want to remember what is working for them.
- When students are struggling and may need to find a skill to help them.
- Whenever students ask.
- *Utilize:* Continuously make the toolbox a part of what you are doing in class.
  - Give students a preview of future learning, so they can be on the lookout for tools that will help them.
  - Allow students to use the toolkit during assessments. (Students love this. They think they are cheating!)

STRATEGY IN ACTION: MOST IMPORTANT POINT (MIP)

At the end of each class period, I have students write down the most important point of the day. To help students determine the MIP, I ask them, "If someone were to ask you 'What did you learn in class today?' How would you answer them?" This is the MIP. The students keep an ongoing list of their most important points. At the end of the unit, they have a comprehensive list of everything they have learned.

I started using this strategy with Writers Workshop. In Writers Workshop, it is important to have a quick five-minute closing where students share what they learned. In my seventh-grade English classroom, the students thrive off of a consistent routine. I was just starting a realistic fiction writing unit and wanted a quick and easy way to see what students understood at the end of each lesson. We were doing a lesson in drafting and how to slow down our story to include more details. At the end of the class, I wanted the kids to write down the most important point. I had the kids take out their notebooks and create an MIP page.

The students, at first, needed some extra help figuring it out. I walked them through the notes they had taken earlier. I asked them, "If an absent student asked what you learned in class today, what would you say?" The students began sharing their ideas, each one building off of the other. Finally, in the end, we had a specific, clear teaching point that all the students wrote down in their notebooks. It looked something like this, "When drafting a short story, it is important to slow down your writing. You can do this by including tiny actions, internal thinking, sensory details, emotions, and purposeful dialogue into each scene."

Overall, students have enjoyed ending class consistently. On the days that we feel rushed at the end, they still ask me, "What about the MIP?" It has been a great way to end class, and I know all the students understood the "why" of each lesson, and they were able to build on their previous learning noted in their MIP pages when I introduce new content and approaches.

—Eleanor Tixier

> ## WHY I LIKE THIS STRATEGY
>
> I like using Most Important Point to help students connect to their previous learning because it is simple, easy, and effective. It helps students reflect on the "why" of the lesson and see how their learning connects when they look at their tangible list of everything they learned in a unit.
>
> —*Eleanor Tixier*
>
> When students develop their problem-solving toolkits, they are actively learning and curious about the connections that we are trying to get them to think about. They engage at a metacognitive level that helps them become agile, creative, and adaptable learners.
>
> —*James Connolly*

Adaptation for Different Assets and Needs

Class Time

Limited Time
* Making connections doesn't need to take much time. You can plan to weave this into your lessons by pausing to emphasize knowledge or skills that are being transferred from previous learning.
* Reduce the number of times students keep track of their learning to once or twice a week.

Lots of Time
* Give students time to create a visual timeline of their learning for display in the classroom.
* Invite guest speakers to talk about the knowledge and skills they apply in their careers.

Technology

Low Tech
* Use paper and pen to keep track of connections.
* Create classroom visuals that reinforce connections.

High Tech
* Develop a Google Slide or other template for students to use when beginning to record connections.
* Use Padlet with each lesson being a different page and each student having a different sticky note.

STRATEGY IN ACTION: TOOLKITS

During the 2021–2022 schoolyear, we challenged students to design their own toolkits based on knowledge and skills they thought they needed to be successful learners. The students began designing and populating their toolkits during the first weeks of school. They thought about knowledge and strategies that had served them well in the past and put them into their toolkits. Many students chose to utilize binders, sheet protectors, and so on, while others created all digital toolkits. Over time, the students who had designed "hard copy" toolkits began adding digital resources to their toolkits by printing QR codes and pasting them into appropriate sections of the toolkits.

The students were very eager to populate each section of their toolkits. Not only did they draw on their previous learning to support their current success, they considered where the gaps were in their learning and independently sought information to bridge those gaps. At times, they looked ahead at content that had not yet been introduced, and considered how their present learning would support their future learning. Additionally, students began engaging in structured and unstructured conversations with one another about the contents of their toolkits. This led to opportunities for students to share (and link) resources.

One of the big takeaways from this experience was witnessing the unexpected ways that the students engaged in completing the task. Their creativity and willingness to revise and reimagine their toolkits was incredible. The toolkits became valuable formative assessment tools for teachers and raised some questions for teachers about the disparity between the concepts that teachers believed were most important (or had been given greatest time/value) and the concepts that students identified as most important and most likely to transfer to future learning.

—James Connolly

Chapter 3

Evidence

In this chapter you will find strategies for assessment that will provide evidence of student learning and help you determine next steps in your planning. These include:

- Using **Formative Assessments** to gauge what students know and are able to do throughout a unit of study (Strategy 10).

    Formative assessments allow us to check in and see what students are getting out of the class experience. They allow us to give students nudges, especially when they aren't intrinsically motivated by grades.

    —*Erica Csimbok Unterburger*

- **Creating Effective Rubrics** that clarify expectations, inform instruction, and guide feedback (Strategy 11).

    It's OK to leave strengths on the rubric! Reinforcing strengths builds confidence.

    —*Kelly DeMarco*

- **Planning with Feedback in Mind** to focus on *when* and *how* to provide students with encouragement and support (Strategy 12).

    I'm really trying to get the kids to integrate and digest the feedback in a way that will feed forward to a stronger performance next time.

    —*Rebecca Blouwolff*

- **Student Choice in How to Represent Learning** that gives students options in materials, process, and mode of sharing that works best for them (Strategy 13).

    Students feel excited about activities they get to choose! Students also feel responsible to complete their activity well when they know they got to choose it.

    —*Amanda Koekemoer*

HIGHLIGHTS

- Learn about adapting instruction based on what you learn from evidence gathered in **Formative Assessments** (Strategy 10).
- Discover ways to help students use rubrics to guide the learning process in **Creating Effective Rubrics** (Strategy 11).
- Check out a rubric that is structured so students can note their next steps in **Planning with Feedback in Mind** (Strategy 12).
- Look for ways to ensure individual accountability within group work in **Student Choice in How to Represent Learning** (Strategy 13).

HOW THESE STRATEGIES MIGHT BE ADAPTED BASED ON TEACHING EXPERIENCE

This chapter is focused on gathering evidence of student learning and making pedagogical choices based on what you learn from that evidence. As you examine the strategies presented, consider how your teaching experience may influence your planning choices. Some advice for both early-career and veteran teachers follows.

Early-Career Teachers

Don't be afraid to fail! It's OK if you plan an assessment that doesn't yield the evidence you hoped for the first time. It may take several weeks and iterations to get those desired results. Be prepared to *guide* students toward success by providing additional instruction based on what you learn from the information you gather from assessments.

Veteran Teachers

Use student work from the past to guide your development of assessments. To save time with providing feedback, develop a strong bank of feedback comments based on what you find yourself commonly stating. Use these common statements to inform future instruction.

How to Implement the Strategy at Varied Grade Levels

Elementary	Middle	High
Consider your evidence and assessment through the lens of students newer to academics and their continued personal and social development. When planning, ask yourself: *How can I help students get in the habit of academic talk when discussing their learning? *How can I encourage students to try new ways of representing their learning and to reflect on how they did so they can begin finding out how they learn and share best?	Consider your evidence and assessment through the lens of early adolescence and continued academic development. When planning, ask yourself: *When can I encourage open conversations about how what is happening in adolescence impacts the ways that students navigate different types of classwork (independent, paired, group)? How might this affect the evidence I collect? *In what varied ways might students document their progress (writing, conferencing, etc.) to show how they are approaching, meeting, or exceeding learning goals?	Consider your evidence and assessment through the lens of students who have college and/or careers on the horizon. When planning, ask yourself: *How am I designing assessments that provide opportunities for students to draw connections between their learning and application beyond the classroom? *How might students develop a way to track their progress over the marking period or full year so they can see their growth?

GUIDING QUESTIONS

As you read through this chapter, consider the following:

1. How do I learn what my students know and can do over the course of a unit of teaching?
2. Which elements of learning are most important to gauge?
3. Do my formative assessments help me see areas of progress and potential next steps that students and I can take?
4. When can I take time to highlight student successes throughout a unit of study?
5. In what ways do my rubrics help inform students about where they need to grow *and* how to do so?

STRATEGY 10: FORMATIVE ASSESSMENTS

> Teacher Contributors
> Elyse Hahne, Grapevine Elementary School (TX), Prekindergarten–5th grades
> Erica Unterburger, Matawan Regional High School (NJ), 9th grade

Formative assessments provide opportunities to assess students' understanding and knowledge without the need to complete a final or high-stakes assessment—like a temperature check gauging what students know and are able to do without the pressure of being right or being at a high level of competence. Formative assessments are part of the process of learning and considering next steps.

Strategy Implementation

1. **Apply the unit's learning goals.** Once you have determined your unit's goals and objectives (see *Strategy 6: Determining Learning Goals* and *Strategy 17: Connecting Skills and Content with Students' Lives and Interests.*), start thinking about formative assessments that will show you where students are in their learning. Then use a pre-assessment to gauge students' knowledge and skills to determine what you want to assess and how you want to assess them as you move through the unit.

2. **Choose types of formative assessments.** Explore different types of assessments, and decide which assessments will best help you gather evidence about different learning objectives throughout the unit.
   - *Daily/Informal:* These are assessments that are done on a daily basis (or close to it), are often built into your routines, and can be used quickly. When coming up with these quick assessments, think about how your students stay connected to what they are learning and respond to feedback. Usually, these quick assessments are used to gauge students' understanding of content or their confidence in skills they are learning. Select the best daily/informal assessments based on what you believe your students will respond to on a consistent basis. Also consider whether the assessment is done as a whole class, in small groups, or individually. Sample daily/informal assessments include:
     - *Thumbs Up/Thumbs Down:* Students raise their thumbs up to show understanding or confidence or thumbs down to show need for more support. They can also point their thumbs somewhere in the middle.
     - *Emoji*: Students select from a group of emojis to represent their understanding or confidence.
     - *Weather Report:* Have students write down the type of weather that represents their understanding of the material or skill.
     - *Conversations*: Simple conversations with individuals, groups, or the whole class with guided prompts (see "On-the-Spot Assessment Ideas") that gauge student understanding.

- *Exit Tickets:* Give a prompt at the end of class that has students record their understanding of the big ideas for the day that you collect (and discuss if you have time).
- *Slap Out:* Students place a sticky note on a piece of paper by the door that has three categories: Got It, Need More, and Feeling Lost.

On-the-Spot Assessment Ideas

Effective on-the-spot assessment takes planning. Consider what information to gather that will help you determine future instruction and assessment.

- What to listen for:
    - Where are students in the progression of reaching the objective?
    - How are they processing information?
    - What types of clarifying or probing questions are they asking?
    - How ready are they to move on to what is next?
- Providing feedback on works in progress:
    - How well does the work (in its current state) meet the objective?
    - What needs clarifying?
    - What is well explained?
    - How well organized is their work?
    - What next steps are needed?
- What to ask your students:
    - Explain this to me.
    - Tell me the gist of what we've been talking about.
    - What do we know about . . . ?
    - How do we . . . ?
    - How do you use this learning?
    - How does this apply across subjects?
- What to ask yourself about student work:
    - Which students are keeping up with the pace and engaged?
    - Whose answers are off base?
    - Who isn't sharing but has great stuff written?
- What to ask yourself about next steps:
    - Do I need to reteach?
    - Do I need to monitor and adjust?
    - Can we move on?

When we plan, my co-teacher and I look for moments where there will be opportunities to check in.

—*Erica Csimbok Unterburger*

- *Traditional versus Creative*: It's important to vary the types of assessments that you use. Some students are comfortable with more traditional formative assessments such as multiple-choice or short-answer quizzes. Others prefer to show their understanding of content and application of skills in more creative ways. Try to plan for a mixture of traditional and formative assessment throughout the unit to help students feel comfortable with the assessments and stretch them in ways to demonstrate their learning. Samples include:
    - *Traditional:* Quizzes, short-answer responses, graphic organizers, outlines, notes
    - *Creative:* Posters, comic strips, podcasts, short videos, fake social media posts
- *Benchmark:* These are formative assessments that are preplanned and aimed to cumulatively assess what students have learned up to that point in the unit. It is useful to create a minimum of one benchmark for every two weeks of a unit (or more if you have time). If you are using more than one benchmark, try to integrate both traditional and creative assessments.
- *Individual/Group/Whole Class:* When planning for assessment, be sure to vary how you gather information. Ideally, you are able to integrate individual and group/whole-class formative assessments during each lesson to learn about the needs of individuals and trends across the class.
    - *Individual:* When you assess individually, you are able to see where each student is in their learning. Ultimately, you need to know where each student is in their learning process.
    - *Group/Whole Class:* When you assess work that has been completed in groups or assess the full class, you may learn important information about trends in overall learning and ideas for next instructional steps. That said, there are ways to assess individual progress through group work by having students self-report their contributions to the group, reflect on their takeaways from the process, or consider how to better contribute to the group in the future.

3. **Adapt plans based on what you learn.** Use formative assessment results to inform adaptations to your plans and meet students where there are.
    - Adapt your instruction plans by:
        - Reteaching information in a new way.
        - Providing more targeted skills practice.
        - Building on connections to students' success in prior units of study, and reminding them that these successes were the foundation for their current learning.
        - Diving deeper into a facet of the unit that is particularly interesting or engaging.
        - Allocating more time for more challenging concepts or skills.
    - Follow up with students by:
        - Reminding them of related knowledge or skills that they have learned before.
        - Sharing how they will use the knowledge and skills in the future.
        - Providing opportunities for them to learn from one another.
    - Revise future formative assessments to:
        - Determine growth in areas where students struggled.

- Build on students' strengths/preferred means of demonstrating learning.
- Provide opportunities for students to demonstrate ways they've extended their learning beyond the unit objectives/goals.

> Learning is cyclical, and it does not look the same along the way. Year to year, concepts and skills become more advanced, and teaching and assessments shift to build on foundations.
>
> —*Elyse Hahne*

4. **Consider readiness for a summative assessment.** Use the information you gather from formative assessments to determine the timing for and adaptations of your summative assessment. Remember that readiness for a summative assessment isn't about perfect scores; it's about students demonstrating their unique understanding and skills development.

> A lot of times our work is driven by curriculum guides. We know the summative drives what we want them to know, but we have to take that formative temperature check before then to be sure they are ready. Are they ready to move on and take that summative assessment or do I need to reteach?
>
> —*Elyse Hahne*

5. **Extend learning.** A summative assessment doesn't have to mean the end of studying a topic. Pay attention to what formative (and summative) assessments reveal about students' interest and engagement with a topic. Ensure students understand how to apply their learning beyond the assessment. Discuss how this transfers to other classes and to future learning in school and life outside of school.

STRATEGY IN ACTION: ADAPTING INSTRUCTION BASED ON FORMATIVE ASSESSMENTS

This year in first grade, we talked about living and nonliving things. We did environmental walks where we asked what do you see that is living? Some students shared "I see grass. It grows, so it is living. These are the things that are not living (rocks, buildings, bricks)." They differentiated between living and not living and wanted to go even further (*what humans need to live and what other living things need to live*). First grade just needed to know living and nonliving, but the formative assessment that arose through discussions and their questions showed that they were ready to move on to a more sophisticated level of classifying living things as compared with humans.

Students changed their T-chart from living versus nonliving to living (animal), living (plant), and nonliving. This showed how much they knew and the depth of their thinking. Students even took pictures of each other and of things they saw on their environmental walk.

Based on one formative assessment, we were able to adapt expectations during the learning process and the ways students were assessed. It should be noted that there was a mix of student ability in this class (gifted and talented, special education, general education); high level questions came from all students.

—*Elyse Hahne*

WHY I LIKE THIS STRATEGY

I like formative assessments because it benefits both the teacher and the student. Formative assessments, in the realm of questioning and wondering, helps the teacher understand what students know as well as gaps in their learning. Students wonder and think aloud giving the teacher ways to see, hear, and observe what students know. I truly believe students benefit from formative assessments as they are a springboard to what they think and wonder about.

—*Elyse Hahne*

Formative assessments allow us to check in and see what students are getting out of the class experience. They allow us to give students nudges, especially when they aren't intrinsically motivated by grades.

—*Erica Csimbok Unterburger*

Adaptation for Different Assets and Needs

Class Size	
Small Class	*Large Class*
*Take more time with each student or group to assess where they are in their learning. *Conference with students about the information you have gathered through formative assessments. Help them see connections to what they have learned or will learn next.	*Plan more small-group formative assessments in place of individual assessments, which will allow for more focused feedback in manageable chunks. *Be efficient with your time by focusing on one or two specific elements in each formative assessment.

Technology	
Low Tech	*High Tech*
*Remember that students need to learn problem-solving without the use of technology. Sometimes low-tech options allow for greater creativity and more options for demonstrating learning. *Create a low-tech checkout process by having students place a sticky note on one of three posters as they leave the room ("Got it," "Need More Time/Practice," "Feeling lost!").	* Be purposeful with what you want to assess and make sure you aren't slipping into assessing computer skills when you mean to assess something else. *Provide guidelines for tech use and plan for ways to highlight ways that students use tech creatively so students can learn from and be inspired by their peers.

STRATEGY IN ACTION: ASSESSMENT REVEALS AN AREA FOR GROWTH

At the beginning of the year, I assign a research project where students need to create a resume for a world leader. I tell high schoolers to find reliable sources to learn about their leader. When I walked around after they had a period to work on this, students were typing their person's name into Google and copying and pasting whatever came out. When I asked about this process, they answered "Oh it's Google." This told me that we had to do a mini-lesson on reliable sources and the difference between a search engine and reliable sources.

I asked the school media specialist to support us in learning about proper sourcing and in developing a set of resources in databases. Together with the students, we discussed what makes the resources within the database reliable. We had talked about this before starting the project, but it became clear that students needed a refresher. They came in with this knowledge of .edu and .gov, but they didn't transfer that knowledge to this research. Through formative assessment, I realized the importance of this refresher and I was able to collaborate with my colleague to provide the support they needed.

—*Erica Csimbok Unterburger*

STRATEGY 11: CREATING EFFECTIVE RUBRICS

> Teacher Contributors
> Kelly DeMarco, Pond Road Middle School (NJ), 6th grade
> Shellyann O'Meally, Western International School Shanghai (China), 4th–5th grades

A rubric can be a powerful tool for clarifying expectations, informing instruction, and guiding feedback. By using the Understanding by Design® (UbD) (Wiggins & McTighe, 2005) frame and encouraging student voice in the development process, teachers can create effective rubrics for all learners.

Strategy Implementation

Part I: A UbD Approach to Rubric Design

1. **Develop rubrics that address learning goals and make clear connections to next steps.** When developing a rubric that supports students' individual learning, focus on specific knowledge, skills, and dispositions (K/S/D) that you want students to demonstrate. Develop descriptors that emphasize the areas of strength in their work and opportunities for growth in relation to the major elements of the assessment. Be concise and clear about what you see in the student work and what you want students to do next. When developing the rubric:
   - *Determine the K/S/D to Assess:* Ponder the *why* behind the assignment and what you want students to demonstrate through it. To help focus your thinking, consider:
     - *Students' Areas of Strength and Needs for Development:* To effectively gauge where students thrive and where they need support:
       - *(If Possible), Meet with Students' Former Teachers:* Talk to students' former teachers to gather insight on prior learning that you can build on and areas of struggle that you can address. This can happen at the start of the year or throughout the year when trying to learn information directly related to specific assignments and projects.
       - *Reflect on Assessments from Prior Units:* Examine formative assessments that revealed trends in student understanding or strengths and areas for growth in their K/S/D.
       - *Pre-assess:* Use a pretest or another pre-assessment to determine how much students know or how well students can do what you are asking. Be sure to let students know that this may be a struggle for them and the expectation is that they don't know much, but to see how students grow over the course of the unit.
     - *Standards:* Determine which standards you are assessing, which might include school, program, or state standards for your content area, for other content areas that relate to the assignment, social emotional learning standards, or standards developed by organizations such as Teaching for Tolerance, the

Asia Society, or Collaborative for Academic, Social, and Emotional Learning (CASEL). For older students, you might also consider elements of major exams that relate to the assignment such as SAT, ACT, AP, IB.

- *Make Clear Connections to Next Steps in Relation to Learning Goals:* When developing a rubric that supports students' individual learning, focus on the areas of strength in their work and opportunities for growth in relation to the major elements of the assessment. Be concise and clear about what you see in the student work and what you want students to do next. Areas to focus on within the rubric include:
  - *Content:* When assessing students on content using a rubric, make sure to:
    - *Be Concrete:* Write descriptors of the levels of performance so students can see that the goals are attainable.
    - *Include Students in Rubric Creation:* Share exemplars of work, and ask students how they would rate the components (developing, meets target, exceeds expectations). Together, develop descriptors of each level of achieving the goals set for the unit.
    - *Add Glow and Grow Statements:* Within the descriptors of each goal, you likely have statements that highlight the strength of students' work or areas for growth. Create a separate section at the bottom of the rubric for focusing on at least one "glow" (a place where the student's work shines) and one "grow" (an area where the student needs to develop). At first, it may be guesswork determining these descriptors, but over time you will note patterns in comments you are making and add these to your comment banks.
    - *Couple the Rubric with a Checklist for Simple Elements:* Some parts of assignments can be checked as either "yes" or "no." Placing these elements on a separate checklist keeps the rubric focused on the major goals of the assessment. Develop a checklist with items such as:
      - Submitted on time.
      - Spell-checked.
      - Showed all work.
      - Included all parts of the assignment.
      - Responded to all components of the prompt.
      - Used class time efficiently.
  - *Style:* Make your rubric reader-friendly. To do this:
    - *Choose Your Words Carefully:* Write out descriptors in student-friendly, first-person-singular statements that are particular to that unit. For instance:
      - *World Language:* I can use highly practiced words and expressions, give simple details, and submit on time.
      - *Science:* I can write a conclusion to my lab report that summarizes the connections between the evidence gathered and my hypothesis.
      - *Art:* I can write an artist's statement about my work that states the important emotions/ideas that I wanted to convey.
    - *Keep It Short and Sweet:* When you have fewer words on the page, everything points back to the things that are key for students to focus on in terms of their learning development.

2. **Determine *how* you will assess.** Think about the design of your rubric and how you can adapt your rubric if students are choosing how to represent their learning. When determining the design and structure of the rubric, consider:
   - *How Many Elements to Include:* When designing rubrics, often less is more. Students need to know the most important elements of the learning experience that they are meant to be representing. Although there is no one magic number for rubric elements, between five and seven (including elements that are familiar like "grammar" or "good use of time").
   - *Format of the Rubric:* When many teachers think of a rubric, they think of a series of boxes with descriptive text for various elements of an assignment that indicate particular levels of success. Rubrics can be so much more! Work with your students to decide which is most helpful. See samples of each type of rubric in *Sample Materials* on page 68:
     ◦ *Standard Rubric:* Each element is broken down across rows of a grid into varying levels of success, from not meeting expectations to exceeding expectations.
     ◦ *Single-Point Rubric:* The descriptor of each element is in the center column; the left column provides room for comments on how the student may grow to better meet that element and the right column has space for comments on how the student has exceeded expectations.
     ◦ *Rating Scale Rubric:* Each element is listed with a list of levels of how well a student has met the criteria. (4: I definitely did this; 3: I mostly did this; 2: I somewhat did this; 1: I did not do this at all). Leave space for students to explain how they believe they met the requirements or what they need to do better.
     ◦ *Developmental Rubric:* Each element is listed with levels of where students are developing the K/S/D for said element such as developing, sufficient, and mastery. Make space on the rubric where you can give advice on each rubric item letting students know how to move to the next level.
     ◦ *Checklist:* Determine the most important elements of the assignment and how students can demonstrate them. (For example, for an argumentative paragraph, you might include a claim, two pieces of evidence, acknowledgment of counterargument, refute counterargument, and closing.) These elements can be listed so students can cross-reference their work with the checklist; they may even color-code or annotate their work to indicate where they met each criterion.

   > It's OK to leave strengths on the rubric! Reinforcing strengths builds confidence.
   >
   > —Kelly DeMarco

   - *Adapting for Student Choice:* If students have options for representing their learning (see Part II), consider whether the rubric needs to be changed to fit each option or whether it can remain the same for all. Typically, when granting student choice, the rubric can remain the same because the elements being assessed should remain consistent, regardless of how students are showing what they

know or what they can do. However, you may want to add space for students to suggest an additional rubric element that represents their efforts. For example:
- *Weighting of Rubric Elements:* Whatever format you choose for your rubric, consider how to weigh each of the elements included. The elements are likely not equal in value in terms of student effort and complexity of thinking. (For example, if you have been focused on following the scientific process with your fourth graders, the grammar in their lab reports may not count as much as the detail in the description of the results.)

3. **Ensure the learning experiences align with the rubric.** Before using your rubric to assess students' K/S/D, consider how well you have set them up for success. Ask yourself, did students' learning experiences align with the assignment and rubric outline? To check for alignment:
   - *Return to Your Standards and Unit Objectives:* See if your lesson plans represent a progression of daily objectives and learning that leads to meeting the larger objectives found in your assignment and rubric.

STRATEGY IN ACTION: USING STANDARDS FOR RUBRIC DEVELOPMENT

One of the New Jersey (NJ) Student Learning Standards for writing is: *NJSLSA. W2. Write informative/explanatory texts to examine and convey complex ideas and information clearly and accurately through the effective selection, organization, and analysis of content.* My grade-level team teacher and I wanted to plan an informational writing unit where students wrote a problem/solution essay on a social issue. Prior to writing, students would be taking notes on articles and videos in a text set (texts chosen for them already) for their social issue. After looking at the NJ standards, we consulted the Writing Pathways continuum as well. We then decided that students needed to be able to exhibit the following skills in their essay: an effective introduction (including a lead and thesis statement), incorporation of evidence from sources, incorporation of their own analysis, an effective conclusion, effective transitions, and finally, editing (capitalization, punctuation, grammar, and spelling).

We took this information and created a rubric that we would use to assess the final essays. Then we worked backward to plan our lessons, deciding on the most effective way to teach each of these skills. We informed students throughout the unit that these skills would be assessed on the final essay, and we let them self-assess/reflect using the rubric we developed, during the writing process and when submitting their final essay. The students were impacted by this strategy because there were no surprises for them; they knew exactly what was expected and what would be assessed. They also learned valuable skills of what needs to be included in this type of essay for future writing endeavors.

—Kelly DeMarco

- *Reflect on Past Experiences:* Consider what helped students meet the objectives in the past and ways to improve your instruction to help students meet your intended goals.

Part II: Student Input in Rubric Design

1. **Make expectations clear.** Students can have an impactful voice in rubric design when they understand the objectives of the assignment. Be clear about the K/S/D that you want students to demonstrate. When you are clear, students can consider what success looks like and potential elements or adaptations to assignment expectations that will help them to be successful.

2. **Determine best ways to demonstrate learning.** Students may have some great ideas for demonstrating their learning in ways that are nontraditional that can be incorporated into the rubric. Taking time to discuss *how* to represent learning will likely yield more creativity in assignments, greater comfort with being assessed, more student success, and (when students have choice) more variety in student products, thus creating less monotony for teachers when grading.

3. **Integrate student ideas.** Once students are clear on expectations and have ideas of how they want to represent learning, you can develop the rubric together. To do this:
   - Start with the objectives you have already shared.
   - Determine what kinds of rubric works best for the students.
   - Draft the rubric and share with students for feedback and editing.
   - Invite students to draft the rubric as a full class or in small groups and come to consensus on the elements and weighting.

4. **Prepare students to use the rubric to guide the learning process.** As students are engaged in learning, be sure to relate what they are doing back to the objectives. Share the rubric early on so students can recognize how what they are doing relates to where they are headed in terms of assessment. Work with students to check in on progress and to determine any needed rubric adjustments. To do this:
   - *Share Samples:* Provide sample work from previous students or a model you developed yourself, and ask students to assess the work based on the rubric. Discuss:
     - What is done well, and how well-prepared students do these things.
     - Areas for the model student to improve and suggestions for how to do so.
     - Components that the rubric does not address, but perhaps should.
   - *Practice:* Have students practice using the rubric before the final assessment. For instance:
     - *Give a Mock Version of the Assignment:* You might do this as a full class, in pairs, or individually. This mock version can be a simplified version of a full assignment, or you might present components of the assignment at different times (e.g., developing a topic sentence, explaining evidence). Use your

rubric to determine what students are ready for and what they need to develop. Also, pay attention to any changes that will make the rubric a better tool for assessing growth.
- *Engage Students in Peer Review:* Peer reviews are helpful for students to evaluate their work and the rubric to see if it is a reliable tool. Whether students are providing feedback to each other or to their teachers, the following are some helpful guidelines:
  - Be sure your feedback is productive and sensitive to students who might struggle with critiques.
  - Use appropriate, understandable language.
  - Relate feedback to expectations.
  - Provide reasoning for your feedback.
  - Make sure you take time to reflect and follow up on feedback.
  - Stay positive and use feedback to grow.
- *Adapt the Rubric as Needed:* Continue to make adaptations to the rubric based on what comes up as students engage in this process. That said, be sure to stay true to your overall objectives.

WHY I LIKE THIS STRATEGY

Allowing students to make connections to their learning, especially feedback of their learning, is important for making connections to the content. Having students co-construct rubrics with their peers and the teacher allows them increased student agency.

—*Shellyann O'Meally*

When rubrics are well-developed and clearly reviewed before the final assignment is due, there are no surprises to students in terms of grading students' work. They know what will be graded because they are being taught these skills in mini-lessons throughout the unit. They also have a chance to self-reflect/self-grade on the exact rubric the teacher uses. This strategy helps me feel organized; I know what to teach during the unit and what goals students should be hitting because I know what I want the end product to look like.

—*Kelly DeMarco*

Adaptation for Different Assets and Needs

Class Time	
Limited Time *Maximize your time by building on what students already know to help them grow. Show this progression in the assignment and the rubric so students can see areas for potential success (e.g., use what you learned about claims and evidence in your argumentative writing unit when developing your debate outline). *Go over the highest ratings for each element of the rubric so students know where to aim.	*Lots of Time* *Plan to engage students in more modeling and examination of what success looks and sounds like according to the rubric. *Use more time to work with students on rubric development. Help them see connections between past work and future work by examining past and future rubrics (expectations).

Academic Diversity	
Limited Diversity *If students are at approximately the same place in their learning, you can plan for more whole-class review of the rubric and support of skills development in relation to the rubric. To do this, continuously make the different elements of the rubric overt during lessons; this way, each student will see what they are able to do and where they need to grow. *Adapt your rubric to extend student thinking or to meet students where they are if the full class is struggling. You may want to develop multiple rubrics by breaking a larger rubric into multiple parts and using those consecutively (over multiple days) so students can demonstrate their learning progress incrementally.	*Lots of Diversity* *Provide support through one-on-one conferences. *Give opportunities for students to add their own elements to the rubric, so they can build confidence.

STRATEGY IN ACTION: CO-CONSTRUCTING RUBRICS

Two years ago, I entered a fifth-grade classroom as an English-language learner teacher. Working with the homeroom teachers of that grade, we were able to put together a unit on machines. We started by asking, "What is a machine, what can it do?" Students then made pictorial representations of machines. Then we gave feedback. "I see that you know what a pull is, what a wedge is. Next step. Can you explain what a machine is and what it does?" Students had a choice to explain verbally, draw, or make a video.

They self-assessed and received feedback based on a checklist with statements such as: *I know what a machine is. I know what it does.* From there, we moved into how to incorporate machines into daily lives. Then how can you create a machine? Students were given an opportunity to explore. Before they could create the machine, they worked with teachers to create a rubric to help them reflect on their learning. In small groups, they evaluated their designs. Based on what they saw as important, the elements of the rubric they helped develop included: *I was able to work with the group. I was able to design something. I was able to use research about simple machines.*

Two weeks before the summative task was due, they came up with the final rubric. I asked, "Now that you've experienced the stages of the past few weeks, what do you want to see on the rubric?" They worked together to develop a class rubric. They considered questions, such as "How did the field trip to an amusement park impact their designs? How did their research impact their designs? In what ways were they especially creative? How well did they cooperate and collaborate with their small groups?" With this approach, students had a say in how feedback would be focused.

—*Shellyann O'Meally*

Sample Materials

Standard Rubric

Graphing Element	Excellent	Proficient	Developing
Type of Graph Chosen	Graph fits the data well and makes it easy to interpret. (5 points)	Graph is adequate but interpretation of the data is somewhat unclear. (4 points)	Graph distorts the data and/or the data is unclear. (0-3 Points)
Accuracy of Plotting	All points are plotted correctly and are easy to see. (9-10 Points)	All points are plotted correctly. (7 Points)	Points are not plotted correctly, or points are missing. (0-6 Points)
Labeling of X Axis	The X axis has a clear, neat label that clearly describes the units used for the independent variable. (5 points)	The X axis has a label that describes makes somewhat clear the units used for the independent variable. (4 Points)	The X axis is not labeled or is labeled incorrectly. (0-3 Points)
Labeling of Y Axis	The Y axis has a clear, neat label that clearly describes the units used for the dependent variable. (5 points)	The Y axis has a label that describes makes somewhat clear the units used for the dependent variable. (4 Points)	The Y axis is not labeled or is labeled incorrectly. (0-3 Points)

Rating Scale Rubric

Complete the **"Self Score" column**. Score yourself based on the 1-4 points scale.

Criteria	Self Score	Reasons for My Scores
	4 points Yes, I definitely did this. **3 points** I mostly did this. **2 points** I somewhat did this. **1 point** I did this a little or not at all.	
Introduction: I wrote an introduction that started with a **lead** to interest readers and draw them into my essay. I wrote a **thesis** that mentions the problem and solution of my social issue.		
Evidence: I included information from my research in my body paragraphs, such as: facts, numbers/statistics, quoted words, examples, and/or definitions. I correctly **cited** my sources by giving credit to the articles and/or videos.		
Analysis: My analysis includes my own thinking, ideas, and reactions to the subject; these can be questions, comments, feelings, and/or connections. I **did not** use phrases like: *I think, I believe, my evidence states, etc.*		
Conclusion: I wrote a conclusion that circles back to the thesis statement. I also successfully incorporated a "call to action," posed a question, or left the reader with a lasting impression.		
Transitions: I used transitions to show how different parts of my text fit together and to connect ideas. I used transitions to help create sequence and flow.		
Capitalization & Punctuation: I made little to no errors in capitalization or punctuation, so my writing is exceptionally easy to read. All of my sources have proper punctuation & capitalization: article & video titles are in quotation marks AND article & video titles are ALL capitalized.		
Grammar & Spelling: I used resources to be sure the words in my writing are spelled correctly, including names, places, and/or technical vocabulary. I very carefully edited for all items on the Editing Checklist.		

Single-Point Rubric

Grow	Criteria	Glow
	**Art Analysis Rubric**	
	Description Detailed description of the subject matter and/or elements of the work.	
	Analysis Accurate and detailed description of several dominant elements or principles used by the artist and how they are used by the artist to reinforce the theme, meaning, mood, or feeling of the artwork.	
	Evaluation Use of 3-4 criteria to judge the artwork, such as composition, expression, creativity, design, communication of ideas.	

Developmental Rubric

Criteria	Progress	Advice for Next Time
Presentation Skills		
Content Speaker demonstrates a full understanding of the topic.	__Mastery __Sufficient __Developing	
Presence Speaker is loud and clear throughout the presentation, stands up straight, and establishes eye contact during the presentation.	__Mastery __Sufficient __Developing	
Response to Questions Speaker is able to accurately answer most questions posed by classmates.	__Mastery __Sufficient __Developing	

Checklist

Reflect on your self-directed learner skills by placing the ✓ under "no," "sort of," or "yes!"

Self-Directed Learner Skill	No	Sort of	Yes!
I used my **independent reading & writing time** wisely and effectively during this unit.			
I **managed my behavior** so that I remained focused and on-task during independent reading & writing time.			
I **asked questions** if I did not understand what was expected or did not know what to do.			
I **used teacher examples/ mentor texts (student examples)** if I needed help or clarification.			
I organized my time to get my work done by the **deadline**.			
I did my **best work** and put in my **best effort** during this unit.			
I feel that I have **grown** as a reader, writer, and a self-directed learner during this unit.			

STRATEGY 12: PLANNING WITH FEEDBACK IN MIND

> Teacher Contributors
> Kate Sullivan, A.P. Willits Elementary School (NY), Kindergarten
> Rebecca Blouwolff, Wellesley Middle School (MA), 6th/8th grades

When planning with feedback in mind, teachers focus on *when* and *how* to provide students with encouragement and support. Teachers may also design feedback tools that help students determine their own next steps for individual growth. When providing and designing tools for feedback, teachers need to plan how to best support their students in a way that is both developmentally and academically appropriate.

Strategy Implementation

When planning for introducing and supporting the development of Knowledge/Skills/Depositions (K/S/D), it is important to know the goals for student learning, how students can show they have met said goals, and ways to support students on their learning journey to meet those goals. Feedback plays an important role in helping students assess where they are in their learning and where they need to go next. By intentionally structuring lessons to include time for feedback and taking action based on feedback, teachers can help their students meet their learning goals.

1. **Identify the goals of the lesson.** There are many learning opportunities in each of the lessons we teach. When planning with feedback in mind, it is important to determine the most essential K/S/D that you want students to learn. You may use the standards, past experience, grade-level curriculum mapping, or other guides to help outline your plans. (See *Strategy 6: Determining Learning Goals*.) Make sure to develop a clear way to communicate what it means to meet the lesson's goals (e.g., model work, checklists, or rubrics) because you must have an idea of what it means to meet these goals so you can provide feedback and guidance to students as they progress.

2. **Determine the type of feedback.** There are several ways to give feedback, including individual, small group, and whole class. (Note that when meeting with individuals or small groups, be sure that all other students are engaged in meaningful work.) Whatever means of feedback you choose, determine how you will deliver this information (written or verbal) and who will be providing the feedback (teacher or peer). When deciding which type of feedback to provide students, consider:
   - *Individual:* Use this when you have specific questions about student work and want to give students an opportunity to explain their thinking.
   - *Small Group:* Use this with groups of students who are struggling in similar ways. Help them grow together.
   - *Whole Class:* Use this when most of the class needs some clarification or redirection. Also, be sure to highlight positive choices or interesting ideas with the whole class.

- *Peer Feedback:* When peers give feedback, this is an opportunity for both the recipient of the feedback and the person providing the feedback to reflect on their own learning and progress. To provide meaningful feedback, a peer must understand what is expected and how best to meet those expectations. Of course, often peer feedback requires some guidelines to ensure that students are helping each other move forward in a positive way. Begin by modeling how to provide feedback. Then give students the chance to look at each other's work and provide suggestions for how to extend their K/S/D development. Work with students to:
  ○ Focus clearly on the goals of the assignment.
  ○ Determine what will show the ways that students are approaching the goals.
  ○ Develop next steps.
- *Rubrics:* Use a rubric to provide feedback and guide next steps. A rubric is a guide for you to provide feedback to students quickly and succinctly. You may cut down on your grading time by simply circling what works and ways you want students to grow. This saved time means students can get more immediate feedback they can act on. When grading and using the rubric, ensure that you:
  ○ *Stay Focused on the Elements Being Assessed:* It can be easy to get distracted from the set learning goals you are assessing with your rubric. For instance, you may be tempted to fix every spelling or grammatical error or comment of the format of a student's work; however, if those are not agreed-on elements of the assessment, let them go (at least, at first). Focus your energy on what you and your students agreed they would demonstrate.
  ○ *Note at Least One "Glow" and One "Grow" Element of the Student's Work:* It is important to highlight a few glows and grows; if you have a long list of each, pare it down to the two to four most important elements. Long lists of each lose their value.
  ○ *Ensure Your Feedback Leads to Next Steps:* You may include suggestions for how to build on student successes and how to develop K/S/D. You may also ask students to write down their own concrete plan based on your feedback; it can be particularly powerful to ask students to share their plan of action.
  ○ *Revisit Feedback over Time:* When beginning a new learning experience or unit of study, encourage students to refer to their plans for growth and challenge them to be on the lookout for opportunities to develop. Also, ahead of their next assessment, ask them to write down what their improvement focus was. This will remind students to show you their growth in this particular area.

> I'm really trying to get the kids to integrate and digest the feedback in a way that will feed forward to a stronger performance next time.
>
> —Rebecca Blouwolff

3. **Consider the best processes to support your goals.** Students respond to different types of feedback based on their preferred learning style, readiness, and general personality. Some possible guidelines for structuring feedback processes follow:
   - *Students Pose Questions to Frame Feedback:* Research shows that feedback is better received and more likely acted on when the recipient of the feedback asks

for specific information (Muacevic & Adler, 2018). Invite students to pose questions or brag about a point of pride in their learning.
- *Student-Driven Conferencing:* Start a conference by asking students to share one thing they are proud of in their work. Then ask about where they want support. If a student does not have a response for one or both of these requests, read over their work with them and think aloud about what they might highlight.
- *Student Reflections on Submissions:* Create a cover page for student work submissions. Include prompts such as:
  - I am most proud of . . .
  - I would like help thinking about . . .
  - I responded to feedback by . . .
  - Something I want you to know about my work is . . .
- *Student Input:* Develop rubrics with room for student voice. (See *Strategy 11: Creating Effective Rubrics*.)

- *Model the Learning and Feedback Process:* It is important for students to see how *you* as the teacher learn, adapt, change, and grow from feedback. Consider thinking aloud as you write an essay, solve an equation, or compare two sources on a topic and how you ask for and receive feedback to support your learning. When modeling your own learning and feedback process, keep the following steps in mind:
  - *Make Connections to Learning Goals Clear:* The first step in the feedback process is ensuring that you clearly understand the learning goals you are trying to meet. For example, if you are comparing two sources on an event in history, connect this overtly with the learning goals of awareness of multiple perspectives and impact on society today. To do this effectively, it is helpful to have the learning goals posted in a common place in the classroom each day. Also, consider foreshadowing the type of feedback you might need to ensure you are effectively making those intended connections.
  - *Make Mistakes!:* Remember that modeling is about conveying a process. Show students how your thinking and skills develop as you work. Make mistakes; refine and revise; get closer and closer to your goal in steps that students can replicate. If you show them that learning happens in iterations, they will be more likely to be comfortable and open during their process. Also,

---

Model Mistakes as a Form of Feedback

I had a student who took any kind of feedback as criticism. Rather than correcting him, I would model any error that this student made in my own writing. He'd catch my errors and ask, "Why did you do that?" Soon he'd realize that he had done the same, saying, "Oh, we both do that." This simple modification of the feedback process allowed him to focus on the goals rather than the stress of being corrected and opened opportunities for meaningful and long-term application of learning.

—*Kate Sullivan*

demonstrate how and where feedback and different types of feedback help you work through your mistakes and "fail forward." (For more on "Failing Forward" see the first book in our series, *Adaptable Teaching: 30 Practical Strategies for All School Contexts*, 2022.)
    - *Students Give You Feedback:* This provides an opportunity for you to model how to accept and act on feedback. It might be tougher than you think! Remember to put aside your own ego and look for opportunities for your own growth alongside the students. Also, think about asking students to give feedback in different forms (written, verbal, pointed, general, etc.) to model how different types of feedback can be effective in different ways and contexts.
  - *Highlight Student Growth:* Just like modeling your own learning process, use examples of student growth, and how feedback supported that growth, as models. Before sharing student work, remember to always ask students' permission to share. Some tips for doing this are:
    - *Document Growth:* Take photos of student work in progress, so you can display it to the class. Make overt the ways that this work got better based on feedback.
    - *Positive Affirmations:* Shout out when students are making positive choices based on feedback. This may help inspire or refocus peers.
    - *Surprising Examples:* Be open to the great examples that may not look the way you expected but still fit the goals and are just too good not to share.
  - *Make Feedback Purposeful:* According to the Oxford Online Dictionary (2024), feedback is defined as "information about reactions to a product, a person's performance of a task, etc. which is used as a basis for improvement." It is important to stay true to the second part of that definition, "for the basis of improvement." Feedback is meant to give students a sense of how to extend their K/S/D. With that in mind, be sure that you are providing students with opportunities to show the changes they have made based on your feedback, including:
    - Giving chances to revise work.
    - Pointing out when students will next apply their understanding or skills in an upcoming lesson or assignment.
    - Providing students with options for demonstrating their improvement based on your comments.

4. **Develop resources to make feedback explicit and action-oriented.** To keep you and your students focused on the learning goals and to ensure that students have a clear understanding of next steps based on feedback, it is helpful to develop resources that you can use repeatedly.
   - *Checklists:* Creating a list of must-haves can be a simple and effective way of helping students know what they need to do next. If one of the must-haves isn't clearly represented in student work, then they know they need to add it. (See "Identify the goals of the lesson" on page 71 to guide the development of must-haves.)
   - *Comment Banks:* To save you time and ensure that you stay focused on the designated learning goals when giving feedback to your students, develop a list of suggestions that you can cut and paste into comments on electronic submissions

or refer to while conferencing with students. If you do this during a conference, consider coupling this with a Next Steps Organizer, so students have a written list of what to do based on your feedback.

- *Next Steps Organizer:* Ensure that students are prepared to act on your feedback by using a Next Steps Organizer, which makes clear what students should do next to meet their goals based on the feedback they just received. Keep the organizer positive and forward-moving by including ways that students are building on their strengths along with ways you want them to develop (see *Sample Materials*). With younger students who are emerging readers and writers, you may just have them repeat back to you what their next steps will be.

STRATEGY IN ACTION: CONFERENCING FEEDBACK TO GUIDE NEXT STEPS

I conferenced with students when I was teaching a kindergarten writing unit about how-to books. In this unit, students were essentially teaching their reader how to do something. They had to identify something in their expertise, and sequentially write how to do the activity using key vocabulary (first, next, then, last).

In one particular lesson, I modeled how to sequentially list the steps to make macaroni and cheese (always model something student friendly!). I was working with a classified student that was prone to rush through assignments, ultimately sacrificing accuracy for speed. I encouraged him to come to a quieter area of the classroom with me for a one-on-one conference. With a rubric in hand and a clipboard for note taking, we sat and reviewed his writing piece. I asked the student to read his writing aloud to me. As he did so, he naturally paused when he noticed an error. Then we would discuss the error (e.g., forgetting a period at the end of the sentence, not using a capital letter at the beginning of the sentence, not drawing a picture that matches the step), and I would give suggestions about how to improve the writing. Together, we looked at the rubric and drew a smiley face if an element was achieved. When there was something that he needed to correct, he would ask if his correction earned a smiley face on the rubric. Earning these smiley faces made him feel ownership of his work while also taking my feedback into consideration and applying it. At the end of the conference, the student returned to his seat to continue working independently on his writing piece, either adding more details or beginning a new piece.

—Kate Sullivan

WHY I LIKE THIS STRATEGY

Using a well-designed rubric speeds up the personalized feedback process by supplying typical comments about how students *glow* and can *grow*. Students read and understand their feedback and are able to choose a focus for their subsequent work.

—*Rebecca Blouwolff*

I find that conferencing is the best way to provide feedback to students because it creates a more personalized experience with their teacher. It also allows for a stronger teacher-student connection and relationship, allowing the teacher to see areas of interest for the student or areas where students are less comfortable with the material and require additional support. I plan for and structure one-on one-conferences within my lessons because some students that are more reserved feel more comfortable participating and learning this way, rather than in a larger group.

—*Kate Sullivan*

Adaptation for Different Assets and Needs

Class Time

Limited Time
- Use whole-class time to discuss common strengths and areas for growth so you can focus more on individualized feedback during conferences and writing rubric notes.

- Focus on the standards and goals that are most important or relevant, and evaluate a variety of models for meeting those goals. Working from models will likely save time.

Lots of Time
- Add time for small-group conferences during which you scaffold peer-to-peer feedback.

- Engage students in developing the rubrics and descriptors of the ranges for meeting standards and goals.

Class Size

Small Class
- Keep student samples from year to year. This will be important for showing a variety of ways to meet expectations.

- Smaller class sizes may mean more time for individual conferencing. Work with students to determine how to make conferencing time supportive and effective.

Large Class
- Review ways to stay focused when working independently. This will be important when you are conferencing individually or with small groups.

- Make the time for meaningful peer feedback. Model this often, and check on students' next steps to ensure they are based on impactful conversations.

STRATEGY IN ACTION: GLOW AND GROW RUBRICS

I started using this strategy in my middle school French classroom after hearing a *Cult of Pedagogy* podcast about single-point rubrics, learning about "glow and grow" feedback from an X [formerly Twitter] colleague (@MmeCarbonneau), and learning about "feed-forward" from World Language trainer Thomas Sauer. With these ideas bubbling in my head, I drafted a new rubric with a lot less words than before, hoping that it would allow my eighth-grade French students to focus on the key characteristics of our "Novice High" learning target:

- Be mostly understood by someone used to a language learner.
- Use highly practiced words and expressions and add simple details.
- Use simple sentences most of the time, combine phrases to create original sentences, and ask questions when appropriate.

Then I added typical comments (e.g., avoid English/combine short sentences to form longer, more complex ones/varied vocabulary/used a variety of connectors/transition words) in two boxes, called "glow" and "grow." I left room at the bottom for students to set a goal based on my feedback.

When it came time to score the assessment (students wrote letters to Québécois host families about their towns and what they'd like to visit in Quebec City), I was relieved by how little I needed to write in order to provide meaningful and actionable feedback. I challenged myself to "put down the red pen" and avoid marking up every single grammar or spelling mistake in their letters. A few times, I thought of a good glow or grow remark that I had left out, and added it to my rubric document for next time. When I handed back students' letters two days later, they were astounded that they were already scored. They took time to read the feedback because they needed that information in order to complete the feed-forward section. I made a note in my planning book to have them revisit their goals at the end of the term, and before the next writing assessment. The feedback loop had finally begun to close!

—*Rebecca Blouwolff*

Sample Materials

Open-Ended Next Steps Organizer

I'm doing a good job at…

I can build on this by …

I can strengthen my work by…

The next time I get to show my progress is…

I will be sure to include…

Rubric with Next Steps

Français 8
Mme Blouwolff

Nom _____

On-Demand Writing Assessment : Mon Look et mon argent de poche

Performance Target: Novice High I can … • mostly be understood by someone used to a language learner (= my errors with target structures/word order do not interfere with communication) • use highly practiced words and expressions, give simple details • use simple sentences and questions, original sentences, pose basic questions • convey my knowledge a few basic cultural products and practices	Minimal to no evidence of target	Partially meets target, though inconsistent	Novice High Meets target thoroughly	Meets target with consistent evidence of next-higher level
1. I can describe my look	X	-	√	+
2. I can explain how I earn and spend my spending money	X	-	√	+
Teacher Feedback : GLOW			**Teacher Feedback : GROW**	
Easy to understand • Variety of vocabulary •Added details Formed original sentences • Used a variety of connectors •Asked questions •			Hard to understand at times • Practice spelling Use more varied words • Add details Form original sentences Add more connectors • Ask more questions	
Based on the feedback, my goals for my next performance assessment are:				

STRATEGY 13: STUDENT CHOICE IN HOW TO REPRESENT LEARNING

> Teacher Contributors
> Amanda Koekemoer, Thomas Paine Elementary School (NJ), 5th grade
> Susan Oppici, Community Middle School (NJ), 7th grade

Student choice in representing learning means that students are presented with options that have been preselected by the teacher, and they may sample and choose an option that works best for them. The options may be in materials used (e.g., selecting which novel they will read during a novel study), social grouping (e.g., studying alone, with a partner, or with a group), or assignment/assessment type (e.g., presentation, quiz, or project).

Strategy Implementation

1. **Develop choices for materials.** There are many ways to vary choices for materials. Think about the: must-haves; meeting students where they are; and collecting, adapting, and developing multiple materials.
   - *Consider the Must-Haves:* You must have a clear sense of what your students are expected to learn over the course of a unit before determining potential materials. Think about the must-have Knowledge/Skills/Dispositions (K/S/D) within the unit you are teaching and connect with students' interests, readiness, learning preferences, and areas for growth. To do this:
     - *Use District Curriculum as Your Guide:* Look at the K/S/D of each unit. Highlight these and put them in an order that makes sense to you.
     - *Evaluate Grade-Level Standards:* Determine what is applicable to each unit of study.
     - *Examine Required Assessments:* Look at standardized tests or other assessments that your students may need to take. Determine the skills assessed within them.
   - *Meet Your Students Where They Are*: Materials should reflect the needs of your students and help support their growth. Consider:
     - *Paying Attention to What Works with Your Students:* Are they visual, kinesthetic, or auditory learners? Do they like to learn through play, through collaboration? Use this information to develop and choose materials.
     - *Reviewing Former Assessments:* Examine assessments students have previously taken and other evidence of student learning. This will help you better understand where students have thrived with various K/S/D and where they still need to grow.
     - *Talking to Other Teachers:* Discuss strengths and needs with students' former and current teachers.
   - *Collect, Adapt, and Develop Materials:* It is often said, "don't reinvent the wheel." You don't need to create new and authentic materials for every lesson

and unit. Rather, start with what already exists and see how you can make it work for your students.
- *Collect:* Collect as many materials related to your content from the district, colleagues who teach the same material, and materials you have previously used. Look at those materials, and choose materials that are accessible for your students and likely to help them develop the K/S/D you highlighted.
- *Adapt:* Share the materials you selected with your colleagues. For instance, partner with your media specialist, your grade-level colleagues, your math and literacy coaches, or any other support you have in your building. During these conversations, discuss and brainstorm the best ways to adapt existing materials to best support your varied students. Students benefit when teachers work together!
- *Develop and Find New Materials:* Go beyond the textbook! Ensure there is diversity of materials that align with the needs of your students. Start with the existing materials you have adapted, and then to fill in the gaps for materials you still need, come up with new materials. Some great places to find new materials include:
  - *Trade Books:* Look for trade books that relate to the topic students are learning.
  - *Online Resources:* For younger students, plan to have them use *Kiddle* and *Duckster*, which are great age-appropriate search engines, when giving them choice in selecting sources. For older students, you may want to curate a list of sources to choose from if you want to ensure that they are working with reliable information.

Games Are a Popular Choice for Representing Learning

Whether online or in person, students love learning through games. Some tips for using games with students:

- Be sure the game fits the objective.
- Know how you will help students make the connection between the fun and the learning overt. Will you talk about the K/S/D that the game supports before students begin, during, or after they play?
- Plan for game pauses to shout-out great thinking or application of skills. This can help students recognize what they are meant to be doing and it can help refocus students who need it.
- Think about how you will adapt the game as needed. For example, if it is a math game, you might have different levels of difficulty for different groups of students.

2. **Provide choices for independent or group work.** School is social! Students typically enjoy working with one another, especially when they can choose their partners. That said, some students prefer to work alone or with just one other person. The following approaches support student choice in group work:
   - *Base Groups:* Form base groups of four to six students that last for a set period of time (a month, a marking period). Within the groups, students may choose to complete work alone, as pairs, or with the whole group. It is good to have these groups last for an extended time so students can return to them frequently and develop a positive dynamic. Within these groups, students can also decide ways to best represent their learning in different ways. (See our first book in the series, *Adaptable Teaching: 30 Practical Strategies for All School Contexts* for more information on base groups.)
   - *Mix Up Groups Based on Tasks:* Develop different groups for different subject areas or tasks. That way, students have more opportunity and choice throughout the day when it comes to partnering, which may result in new ideas about how students can represent their learning.
   - *Provide Opportunity for Individual Accountability within Pairs or Groups:* Remember when working in groups, not only are students trying to learn content and develop skills, but they are also developing interpersonal skills and dispositions. Provide students with choices in how to share with you how well they are working together.
      - *Color-Coded Work:* Each student in the group has a different color pen or font (if working on a shared document).
      - *Individual Reflection:* Students write one to two sentences describing how they were helpful, neutral, or distracting members of their group and what they will do during the next class if the group is meeting again.
      - *Most Meaningful Contribution:* Students reflect on how they contributed to the group's progress and provide detail on what they see as their most meaningful contribution and why.
   - *Use What You Learn about Group Dynamics for Future Planning:* Take note of how different groups of students work together. Understanding optimal group dynamics will help you plan group work that enables students to thrive in making meaningful choices to represent their learning. Consider:
      - Students that work well together.
      - Combinations that are distracting or negative.
      - Opportunities to create a mix that enables new group "leaders" to emerge.
      - Productive choices that groups make (e.g., Taking turns sharing ideas).
      - Choices that have potential to be productive with a bit of support or tweaking (e.g., Trying a new way of representing work like Canva, but needing to understand the chosen platform better).

3. **Create and introduce assignment and assessment choices.** Stay true to the objectives you are assessing when developing choices in the products students create to demonstrate their learning for the assessment. Students may have options for how they show their growth; however, the elements assessed are determined by

the standards and objectives identified at the start of the unit. That said, additional elements may be added, based on what comes up during the learning.
- *Use an Asset-Based Approach:* Assessment means to sit beside and learn what students know and can do. It is not what most students (and some teachers) think, a way to see what students don't know. With the more positive view of assessment in mind, consider ways to adapt the ways students represent their learning to allow for maximum focus on the desired results. Some examples include:
  - Multiple-choice quizzes with room for explaining answers when students are not sure they are correct.
  - Teacher/Student conferences with focused questions and answers about a reading or topic.
  - Structured presentations to the class.
  - Creative representations like artwork, videos, cartoons, songs, and/or skits.
- *Connect Your Objectives and the Assessment:* Present options for representing learning in a way that is clear and that emphasizes the connection between your objectives and the assessment. For instance:
  - *Menu of Choices:* Create a menu of choices that includes brief descriptions of expectations for each option. (See *Sample Materials*.)
  - *Hyperlink Electronic Choices:* If sharing choices electronically, use a document with hyperlinks to the materials needed for each choice.
  - *Develop "Total Points Options":* Students may select more than one way to represent their learning. Each mode has a certain number of points assigned based on their rigor.
- *Choice Based on Time:* Consider how to give students choices around how time is used:
  - *Goal Setting:* Guide students in setting goals and considering detailed steps they will take to reach their goals.
  - *Map Timing:* Think through and map what you consider to be realistic timing. This way, you are prepared to help students plan.
  - *Adapt for Individualized Timing Needs:* Have a plan for when students' timing doesn't align with the full class.

> Students feel excited about activities they get to choose! Students also feel responsible to complete their activity well when they know they got to choose it.
>
> —*Amanda Koekemoer*

4. **Monitor and guide student choices.** It can be daunting to keep track of student growth when your learners are learning and demonstrating their progress in different ways.
   - *Monitoring Students' Work:* The following tips are helpful for monitoring students' work:
     - *Clipboards:* Use a clipboard with the big idea or skills that you are assessing at the top and students' names on one side. As you circulate the room, list

ratings to represent how each student is doing. Take brief notes on specific evidence to support ratings. Based on what you learn, plan for extension or support for the next day (see *Sample Materials*).
- *Adapt as Needed:* Adjust pacing, depth, and rigor based on what you observe with student progress.

- *Guiding Students' Choices:* The following tips are helpful for guiding students' choices:
  - *Grade Small Sections as You Go:* This formative assessment will help you and students know if their choices match their readiness.

> It's very easy for a student who wants to be invisible to be invisible, so those check-ins along the way are so important.
>
> —Susan Oppici

  - *Keep the Focus on the Objectives:* When developing the assessment product, use students' strengths so they can focus on accentuating their growth in connection with the K/S/D being assessed. For instance, if a student wants to make a hyperlink document but doesn't know how, then that may not be the choice for them; rather, develop an assessment product that highlights their strengths like writing an annotated bibliography.
  - *Provide Direct Feedback in the Moment:* Often feedback is more effective in-the-moment, rather than written comments after students have "completed" a task.
  - *Encourage Students to Assess Themselves:* Let them know that you will only look at their work after they have compared it with a checklist or reviewed it using an answer key and made corrections in another color.

WHY I LIKE THIS STRATEGY

This strategy gives students power and buy-in to their work. They are able to work to their strength while also working to improve their areas that they might need to develop. When students have choices, they are more likely to work harder and stay focused.

—*Susan Oppici*

Allowing for student choice shows students that there are a variety of ways to learn and to present their learning; it helps them self-reflect about how they like to learn and try different ways that they might learn. I have found that my classes have been more responsible, independent, empathetic, and mature than classes that are not treated as responsible thinkers who can make choices for themselves.

—*Amanda Koekemoer*

STRATEGY IN ACTION: LITERATURE CIRCLES

I recently moved to teaching fifth grade from teaching first. In first grade, guided reading was a big part of literacy instruction. In fifth grade, I found that most teachers complete a novel study as a whole class and do not assign individual reading. I knew that I needed to incorporate choice into reading as I had done in first grade during independent reading time, but I also wanted to make sure students were reading books that were appropriate for their reading level. I conducted quick running records and found a great number of my students reading below level. The novel study that was normally done in fifth grade would be about two grade levels above their current reading level. I talked to our school's literacy specialist, who suggested literature circles. I took her advice and selected four or five books on each students' reading level and told students we would have a "Book Tasting" where they would have time to sample each book. The day of the book tasting, I set a book on desks and tables around the room. I labeled each book with its level. I gave students a "menu" and wrote two levels they could choose from. Students were so excited and took their task very seriously. Afterward, they wrote down three books they loved, and the literature circles were formed!

Each day, I used a novel I selected for our reading mini-lessons, and then I sent students off to independently read a chapter from their literature circle's book and practice the skill taught during the mini-lesson. Afterward, they jotted notes in their reading journal, and finally, they met with their literature circles and discussed. The discussions were on-task, provided stimulating discussion as students had different viewpoints and opinions, and I was able to quickly assess each student's grasp of the comprehension skill we studied that day as I read their journal entries while they wrote and sat in on their discussions. Groups worked together to make group norms, or a "constitution," which they reminded one another of as needed (especially, "Don't read ahead!"). There was always 100 percent engagement, and students often reflected that the best part of their day was the literature circles.

—Amanda Koekemoer

Adaptation for Different Assets and Needs

Student Personality	
Reserved	*Outgoing*
*Provide options to share work with small groups or one-on-one rather than with the whole class.	*Offer multiple options in which students can use their performative skills.
*Create class surveys, rather than class discussions, to collect data so quieter students feel comfortable sharing.	*Integrate more opportunities for students to collaborate with their peers.

Technology	
Low Tech	*High Tech*
*Design your own games that relate to your objectives. Use playing cards, make whiteboards with sheet protectors, go outside and use sidewalk chalk. There are so many ways to get creative with this!	*Look for online games that relate to your objectives. Offer these as choices for your students and give them time to engage with each possible game.
*Today's students are more likely to want to use a tech-based option. In your plans, highlight the importance of using pen and paper at times so they develop the organizational skills related to this medium.	*Students might miss doing pen and paper work (creating a poster, etc.), so find opportunities to integrate this into your lesson.

> **STRATEGY IN ACTION: DEEP DIVES**
>
> I had a student who was a history buff and knew more about some topics in history than I did. He would tell me if he had a strong grasp of a unit and I would give him the end-of-unit assessment. If he did well on the assessment, he would not complete the unit with the class. Instead, he would choose an area of the unit to dive into more deeply. We would brainstorm what the output would be. He usually had to share his work with the class.
>
> This student was twice exceptional; he was gifted and classified. Since he struggled with executive functioning, the output was tailored to develop those areas. We worked to make sure his presentation was organized and completed in a logical, timely manner.
>
> This student had the power to decide which units he wanted to test out of, how he would conduct his research, and how he would represent his learning. All of this choice allowed him to build on his strong historical knowledge and interest while working on the executive functioning skills he lacked.
>
> Having choice kept him motivated throughout the unit. If he were in class, sitting through information and activities he had already mastered he would have become a behavioral challenge and he wouldn't have had the opportunity to expand his learning through his independent research. Instead, he remained engaged and productive in a way that was meaningful to him throughout the unit.
>
> —*Susan Oppici*

Sample Materials

Book-Tasting Instructions and Organizer

Welcome to our Book Tasting!

How to sample

1. Choose a table.
2. Pick a book that is on your level.
3. Look at the:
    - front and back covers
    - inside flap
    - font
    - illustrations
4. Read a few pages of the book.
5. Think about what you observe. Fill out reflection in your pamphlet.

Welcome to our Book Tasting!

First Course	Second Course	Third Course
Name _____	Name _____	Name _____
Title _____	Title _____	Title _____
Author _____	Author _____	Author _____
Genre _____	Genre _____	Genre _____
First impressions _____ _____ _____	First impressions _____ _____ _____	First impressions _____ _____ _____
Rating OK 1 2 3 4 5 REALLY WANT TO READ	Rating OK 1 2 3 4 5 REALLY WANT TO READ	Rating OK 1 2 3 4 5 REALLY WANT TO READ

Skills Tracker

Skill _____   Date _____

Evidence of Skill in Today's Lesson: _____

Student Name	Developing	Meets Expectations	Exceeds Expectations

Chapter 4

Planning for Instruction

In this chapter you will find strategies for planning for instruction. While determining desired results and developing or working from evidence also relate to instruction, this chapter focuses on strategies that frame daily lessons/units. These include:

- **The Story of Your Lesson(s)**, which ensures there is a coherent narrative arc to your daily teaching (Strategy 14).

    > Preserving the flow from lesson to lesson isn't just about students remembering what happened—it's about getting students back in the atmospheric tone of the class and helping them wash away what they were going through before entering the classroom.
    >
    > —Heather Rippeteau

- **Incorporating Routines into Your Plans** that provide structure and focus student energy on learning (Strategy 15).

    > Being strategic and intentional with routines and structures has allowed for deep learning in my classroom. Students know what to expect within a given routine, so as a class we can focus on everyone's thinking and ideas.
    >
    > —Emily Workman

- **Lesson Pacing** to help students take in information at an accessible rate (Strategy 16).

    > It's rare that students will be both confused and bored. Routine helps eliminate confusion and can be a "win" for them because they always know what to do and how to do it, and novel activities help eliminate boredom.
    >
    > —Heather Weck

- **Connecting Skills and Content with Students' Lives and Interests** to enhance learning and engagement (Strategy 17).

    > Connecting the skills and content with students' lives and interests helps students feel that "my teacher cares" from the very beginning of the year.
    >
    > —Nita Luthria Row

- **Intentional Groupings and Designing Group Work** to challenge students and support their success (Strategy 18).

   > Classrooms tend to be hierarchical where the teacher is usually the main figure who guides the class and the students listen and then complete the task. With intentional grouping, the students are key actors.
   >
   > —*Alisa Ettienne*

- **Considering Equity and Multiple Perspectives** in how the curriculum is framed, texts are selected, assessments are created, and the types of activities are planned. (Strategy 19).

   > It's not just about reading and writing, it's about understanding cultural differences related to emotions, roles, etc. Kids often carry quite a bit from home and then you as the teacher can support them.
   >
   > —*Akiko Mazor*

- **Using Learning Management Systems to Organize Your Lessons** and keeping information in one place for educators, students, and parents/guardians (Strategy 20).

   > Using a LMS puts everything on a platform where you are creating online teaching materials, not just for students, but also for families at home to see and be able to support their children when needed.
   >
   > —*Jeff Bradbury*

HIGHLIGHTS

- Explore ways to build cohesiveness between lessons and units in **The Story of Your Lesson(s)** (Strategy 14).
- Learn about a Problem-Solving Workshop routine in **Incorporating Routines into Your Plans** (Strategy 15).
- Discover how to balance structure and surprise in **Lesson Pacing** (Strategy 16).
- Read about how to adapt plans by applying what you learn about students in **Connecting Skills and Content with Students' Lives and Interests** (Strategy 17).
- Consider how to use knowledge of your students for **Intentional Groupings and Designing Group Work** (Strategy 18).
- Learn how to select inclusive texts in **Considering Equity and Multiple Perspectives** (Strategy 19).
- Read about how to provide feedback on the go in **Using Learning Management Systems to Organize Your Lessons** (Strategy 20).

Planning for Instruction

HOW THESE STRATEGIES MIGHT BE ADAPTED BASED ON TEACHING EXPERIENCE

This chapter is focused on planning for instruction. As you examine the strategies presented, consider how your teaching experience may influence your planning choices. Some advice for both early-career and veteran teachers follows.

Early-Career Teachers

Be sure to block time for planning and do your best to stick to that allotted time. To help you be efficient, take advantage of newer resources and strategies you have been exposed to and reach out to veteran teachers who have expertise in the elements of instruction described in this chapter. Be sure to incorporate varied approaches so you can find strategies that work for you and your students, and to keep things interesting.

Veteran Teachers

Push yourself to keep reevaluating the best approaches for your units and lessons, to deepen your knowledge and resources, and to try new strategies that enhance the pacing and engagement in your classroom.

How to Implement the Strategy at Varied Grade Levels

Elementary	Middle	High
Consider your instructional choices through the lens of students new to academics and their continued personal and social development. When planning, ask yourself:	Consider your instructional choices through the lens of early adolescence and continued academic development. When planning, ask yourself:	Consider your instructional choices through the lens of students who have college and/or careers on the horizon. When planning, ask yourself:
*How do my plans encourage my students to learn about one another and build relationships that enable them to work together in meaningful ways? *In what ways do I provide a balance of novel experiences and routines to build their knowledge, skills, and dispositions?	*How will the varied approaches I am incorporating be received by students who are in different phases of adolescent development? How does their maturity impact their readiness for what I hope to do? *How do I support cultural awareness and sensitivity throughout all of my approaches?	*In what ways can I share varied approaches to enhance students' awareness of how they learn best and what distracts them from learning? *What learning habits do students need to develop and refine to be lifelong learners?

GUIDING QUESTIONS

As you read through this chapter, consider the following:

1. In what ways do my lessons and units follow a story arc and pacing that lead to student engagement and success?
2. Which routines afford more time and energy dedicated to learning in my classroom?
3. In what ways can intentional grouping and group work provide autonomy and opportunities for students to develop?
4. How can I grow in developing more equitable representation and learning in my classroom?
5. How do I use learning management systems in ways that benefit me, my students, and their families?

STRATEGY 14: THE STORY OF YOUR LESSON(S)

> Teacher Contributors
> *Morena Christian, Escuela Campo Alegre (Venezuela), Kindergarten*
> *Heather Rippeteau, Millennium Brooklyn High School (NY), 9th grade*

Like an author constructing all the aspects of their novel or a beautifully crafted essay, the teacher creates student experiences through a narrative lens that integrates the unit/lesson content and skills. There are many things a teacher cannot control, but how they construct the flow of tasks, the way each piece of content is revealed, and the scaffolding and progression of skills all contribute to how students experience the overall unit or lesson. NOTE: Telling the story of your lesson(s) applies to the overall story you are telling within your entire unit.

Strategy Implementation

1. **Understand the parts of the story.** Great stories and lessons should include the following elements:
   - *Beginning:* There are three important elements to the start of any great story or lesson:
     - *Hook:* Find a way to catch the attention of your students with a prompt that is meaningful to them and can connect directly to the goals and content for the day.
     - *Context/Background:* Use the hook to transition to providing the larger context and background for the goals and content for the day. Set the stage for the day and situate the lesson or story within the larger context of what students have been learning up to that point.
     - *Purpose:* After providing the context, lay out the goal(s) for the day that students will be able to achieve by the time they complete the day. This might be an "aim" for the day, an agenda with explanation of why students will be engaging in each step, or a focus question that encompasses the day's learning.
   - *Middle:* Once you have laid out what you will be doing for the day, you need to strategically build toward helping your students meet the lesson's goals.
     - *Build Your Story/Argument:* It is important to consider how to sequence your story/argument in a logical way that helps students understand the foundational elements of the content and skills and then can work toward applying what they have learned. You can have lots of great parts of your story or lesson, but if they are not ordered in a way that they build off of one another, the lesson can become confusing and not allow the main ideas and content to be effectively retained.
     - *Seamless Transitions:* To help connect the parts of the story/lesson, you need to create explicit transitions that explain how one part of the lesson is directly connected to the next part of the lesson. If it is difficult to come up with a transition connecting parts of your lesson, then it means that you need to

reorganize the parts of the lesson to a more logical sequence or come up with new parts of the lesson that make more sense.
- *End:* Every great story and lesson needs a solid closure.
  - *Closure/Wrap Up:* At this point, the story and lesson should have given the students enough information to reach your goal(s) for the day; it just needs to be explicitly brought back to those goals. Therefore, find a way to take what students have learned and tie it directly back to the purpose.

2. **Have clearly defined goals.** Start with goals that capture what you want your students to know and be able to do by the end of the lesson. The goal should be one that frames how the story of your content and skills for the day will be told.

3. **Align lesson goals with content, skills, and experiences.** With the lesson's goals in mind, select content, skills, and experiences or activities that directly align with the lesson's goals. If the content, skills, or experiences don't align with the goals, you need to either adapt goals or your plan. For example, if the aim of the day is to connect characterization and setting and you plan to have students make posters about characters, be sure that an element of those posters relates to setting and how setting influences characterization.

Factors that Impact Your Lesson Story
• Texts and tasks
• How the material is presented
• Language used by teacher and students
• Teacher disposition and reactions
• Emotional tone of the classroom

4. **Find your story.** Determine the best way to situate the content, skills, and experiences to tell a cohesive story—with a clear beginning, middle, and end—within the lesson. The lesson story should build on what students learned from previous lessons in the unit while setting things up for the story of subsequent lessons. Together, each lesson's story should be sequenced in a way to tell the larger story of the unit. To do this, ask yourself:
   - *What Do You Want to Teach?:* Think about all of the content skills you want your students to learn for the day and determine:
     - *Content:* What content are you meaningfully able to cover within the time frame to successfully help students meet the day's goal(s)? How does the different content fit together to tell the best story?
     - *Skills:* Select one to three skills to help your students develop throughout the lesson that can be taught and aligned well with the content for the day.
   - *How Do You Want to Teach?:* Once you have determined what you need to teach, it is important to figure out the best way to convey the material to make it engaging and meaningful for your students.
     - *Experiences:* Consider how you want to teach the content and skills through experiences or activities that are meaningful to the students. Try to build from foundational experiences to application experiences and mix up whole-class, small group, pair, and individual work so students have different ways to

experience what they are learning and make their own meaning and connections to the material and goal(s) for the day.
- *How Do You Sequence the Lesson to Tell the Best Story?:* After the experiences are planned, organize them in a way that helps the content and skills build toward answering the goal(s) for the day. Then test whether the sequencing is logical, write transitions between the experiences; if they flow and make sense and you believe students will be able to meet the lesson goal(s) by the final experience, then you likely have a solid sequence. Note that your sequence does not need to be the same as a colleague's; what is important is that you are able to clearly articulate the flow of the lesson and story to your students, even if it is told differently than a colleague.

STRATEGY IN ACTION: KEEPING RHYTHM AND ROUTINES IN THE STORY FLOW

The story of my lessons always come from the rhythm and routines I set up for each lesson. I start by thinking about the objective of the lesson and skills needed to develop (e.g., vocab, oral, writing, reading skills). Then every lesson needs to start with a motivator that gets them enthusiastic about the lesson and gets them engaged (like a video). Try to find the best videos or create your own that will definitely engage all of the students. It's not presenting for the sake of presenting. What's the purpose of showing the video? You want them to love it and want to participate! You want them to ask to do something over and over again because they love it.

Then you want to think about how you develop the skills after you provide that motivation through the following activities! To do that, I focus on finding a flow in the lesson that is easy for students to understand and follow and keeps them engaged and focused on what they are learning, while reinforcing what they have done. You are also having students continually reexplain what they have done. It takes time to help students get used to these routines and rhythm of the lesson.

—*Morena Christia*

Building Cohesiveness between Units

I always think critically about ensuring what students are learning from unit to unit has a spiral nature to it where they are getting to practice and build a little bit at a time. I am also thinking about the emotional tone of the classroom from unit to unit, which is often dictated by the texts, and paying close attention to skills and ensuring they are gently building on each other so students can experience success as they learn each skill and build on each skill.

—*Heather Rippeteau*

> **Make It Interdisciplinary**
>
> Planning needs to be considered in relation to students' other subjects to make what they are learning more interdisciplinary. This way you are reinforcing what students are learning across subjects and looping back, making it one larger story for them.
>
> *—Morena Christian*

5. **Make it engaging.** Ideally, your lesson story should go beyond what students learn and be about something they love and are engaged with. Go back through the experiences you have planned to tell your story and adapt any experience to ensure most students will feel connected to what they are doing and learning. (See *Strategy 17*:

> **WHY I LIKE THIS STRATEGY**
>
> If the teacher doesn't think about the story of their lesson(s), the learning becomes a waste of time. If they don't think about the objective and purpose, it's really hard to differentiate and figure out what you want students to achieve. Without the connections, the flow, and the differentiation, the learning doesn't work or stick with the students. When there is a flow and interaction and good planning and good objectives, then the teacher finds ways to help students relate what they are learning to what they have previously learned and what they need to learn.
>
> *—Morena Christia*
>
> There is nothing like listening to a good story with a great storyteller. People have loved community storytellers since the earliest human settlements and now is no different. Every lesson is like a chapter in the story of a unit and each chapter gives you a little more information on the world you are studying and getting to know, gives you a chance to navigate that world a little more skillfully. I feel it is a privilege to curate a young person's knowledge of the world, to be a part of shaping their worldview, and I do my best to show how seriously I take that responsibility by spending time crafting lessons in this way.
>
> In a perfect world, the unit is an experience for students and part of that is making sure that you are connecting all the pieces as you move through the experience so that when students talk to each other and their families, other teachers, etc., they can reiterate what they have been learning, that there's enough of a throughline to retell what's going on in their classroom.
>
> By integrating storytelling into each lesson, you get that advantage of validating how people experience stories, especially in this world where students experience stories through YouTube, TikTok, podcasts, and at the dinner table. One of my strengths as an educator is performing and drawing in the audience, so the narrative is built into how I prepare for working with my students.
>
> *—Heather Rippeteau*

Connecting Skills and Content with Students' Lives and Interests for ideas of how to do this.) The more engaged students are in each experience, the more they will stay focused on the lesson's story from beginning to end.

6. **Check the flow.** Once you have shaped the story of your lesson, you need to ensure it has the optimal flow. To do that, check that there is:
   - A direct connection to the day's previous lesson.
   - Smooth and logical transitions between each part of the lesson.
   - Building and application of skills and content as the lesson progresses.
   - A conclusion that connects to the theme and goals for the day.

Preserving the flow from lesson to lesson isn't just about students remembering what happened; it's about getting students back in the atmospheric tone of the class and helping them wash away what they were going through before entering the classroom (bad math test, drama with friends, etc.), helping students emotionally reset.

—*Heather Rippeteau*

Personalize the Story

Once the lesson/unit is written and I'm reviewing it prior to teaching, this is where I think about ways to connect to specific students or sections, which celebrities, pop culture, or current event references are relevant for the lesson so that the tone of the classroom follows the tone of the content or skill we're working on. The goal is to ensure that the experience feels like time well spent—laughter, venting, mistakes, memory-making moments are all part of that. To a certain extent, I can prepare to make that magic happen in the room.

—*Heather Rippeteau*

---

7. **Make the story visible and explicit.** After you have planned the lesson story, create materials that allow your students to follow the story throughout the lesson. This includes:
   - *Slides:* Create a slide deck where each slide includes:
     - *Activity:* The instructions for the activity are clearly broken down into its parts.
     - *Timing:* Predicted timing is clearly written down for each part of the activity.
   - *Transitions:* You can add slides that help move the story forward and help students see how the next part of the lesson builds off of what they just learned.
   - *Talking Points:* You can add talking points to the notes in your slides or add them directly to the slides for the students to see. The purpose of these is to ensure you are verbally letting students know how the story flows. They also offer reminders about the tone of the lesson, important anecdotes to share, and reminders about language usage and trigger/content warnings for specific or general students.

8. **Tone and personalization.** Think about how you can bring your own personality into the lesson and set a tone that aligns with the needs of your students and each class you teach. It is important to adapt and match the tone to vibe of each class. This might result in using different jokes or humor from class to class, integrating different images, videos, or texts, or shifting how you tell the story of the lesson, even though the overall goals, story, and experiences are mostly the same.

**STRATEGY IN ACTION: USING THE STORY OF
YOUR LESSONS TO PLAN THE UNIT**

I was planning to teach a new novel that discusses the challenges of modern migration through the story of two main characters but also through many other migrants that appear in vignettes throughout the novel. The unit also coincided with National Poetry Month, and I had several collections of poets who write about their migration experiences. My goal was to have students create a final piece that would demonstrate the connections between the migration experiences in the novel and the migration experiences in the poems (both works of fiction but also nonfiction in that they are real life experiences).

I used the strategy of "the story of my lessons" to plan the unit. Although I built the lessons for the novel (character development, writing style, diction, narrative choices, symbolism), I also carefully curated poems from each poet's collection into a primer, and then strategically wove them into the unit, so that there would be a way to pause at moments in the novel and reflect on the experiences of migration, but through the voice of a poet. Additionally, it helped tell the smaller stories within each lesson that wove together to tell the unit's larger story.

This unit was a progression from the previous unit where we were studying *Macbeth* and focused a great deal on Shakespeare's ability to describe troubling circumstances in beautiful language. It was also a forward-looking unit because our next novel, *Homegoing* by Yaa Gyasi, is about migration and character development and what it's like to be in a new place. So I made sure I retained a natural flow from one unit to the next so students could see how they all tied together.

—*Heather Rippeteau*

Adaptation for Different Assets and Needs

Curricular Freedom	
Limited Freedom	*Lots of Freedom*
*Take whatever curriculum you are mandated to use, and find the best way for *you* to tell the story. Every content has a story in it; it is just how you decide to frame and tell it. *Supplement the mandated curricula with additional texts, videos, and other resources to tell the larger story you want to convey. Most schools will allow additional materials if you cover everything you are required to use.	*Determine the stories you want to tell and then intentionally select materials that directly align with those stories. *Build in student choice in selecting materials for each unit and provide options for student assessments that are meaningful and engaging for them.

Planning/Class Time	
Limited Time	*Lots of Time*
*Go lesson to lesson and week to week and make sure that you're helping students return to the story you are telling at the beginning and end of each class and week (within the unit). *Assign a job to students to plot what is happening from day to day (aim, content, important conflict in history/book or skill, etc.), and put a poster on the wall to plot it. Then it's a good record for the next year if you're teaching the same course again.	*Plan out the entire course as a large story that you then break into unit stories and then lesson stories. Begin this process before the school year and then use your prep periods throughout the year to tweak and realign the larger and smaller stories to retain a cohesive narrative for your students. *In addition to having students plot what is happening from day to day, have students add connections to prior learning and predictions about future learning.

STRATEGY 15: INCORPORATING ROUTINES INTO YOUR PLANS

> Teacher Contributors
> Margaret Summers, Belvedere Elementary School (VA), 5th grade
> Samantha Altman, River Dell Regional High School (NJ), 9th–12th grade

Planning and incorporating routines into your plans include everything from what students do when they enter the room to how they structure classwork and conversations to how they reflect at the end of the class. These routines provide consistency that enables students to direct their energy toward learning rather than logistics.

Strategy Implementation

1. **Use class time purposefully.** Think about and list the overarching goals of your lesson (see *Strategy 6: Determining Learning Goals*). Then consider how to meet those goals within the different parts of your lesson (see *Strategy 14: The Story of Your Lesson(s)*).
   - *Divide into Time Blocks:* Determine the purpose of each part of your lesson. For example:
     - *Beginning:* Provide opportunity for students to get settled and focused; check in with students to determine readiness for learning; call on prior knowledge; introduce expectations.
     - *Middle:* Introduce new concepts; model processes; give time for exploration, practice, or application individually or in groups.
     - *End:* Reflect on what was learned; assess strengths and areas for growth; preview what is coming next.
   - *Be Efficient and Impactful:* Find efficient and impactful approaches to engage students in using each chunk of class time purposefully. For instance:
     - *Beginning*
       - Engage in grounding through shared breathing, a quiet moment, or sharing a quote of the day.
       - Check in with students through a question of the day, a mood meter, or an online survey.
       - Call on prior knowledge by asking a student to review a topic, sharing exit slips from a previous lesson, or posing questions to guide students to remember key information.
       - Introduce expectations with a focus question or aim on the board, a class agenda, or challenge statement.
     - *Middle*
       - *Teacher-Centered:* mini-lesson, interactive lecture, modeling, Socratic questioning
       - *Student-Centered:* individual work, group work, stations, projects
     - *End*
       - Ask students about their learning (see "Most Important Point" in *Strategy 9: Connecting with Previous Learning*)

- Determine knowledge, skills, or dispositions (K/S/D) that need support/reinforcement.
- Preview related upcoming learning experiences.

2. **Determine logistics for approaches you will regularly use.** There are multiple logistics to determine, including:
   - *Student Location:* Consider where the students will be located:
     - Beginning: Will students begin at their desks or in a "meeting area" like a classroom rug?
     - Middle: Will this routine involve desk work, flexible seating, groups, or stations?
     - End: Will you reflect or wrap up from desks, stations, or meeting area?
   - *Materials:* Think about what materials students need. Additionally, ask yourself:
     - Where will the materials be?
     - Will students gather them for themselves? Will they be at their desks?
     - Is there a group "materials gatherer"?
     - What are the procedures for putting materials away?
   - *Learning Environment:* Determine the optimal environment to help facilitate student learning. This might include choices like:
     - Lights on or off.
     - Music or quiet.
     - Flexible or assigned seating.
   - *Flexible versus Fixed Elements of Routines:* Think about which routine elements should be flexible and which elements should remain constant. Some of these elements might include:
     - Timing
     - Noise level
     - Location
     - Order of steps in the routine

> When you make your routine, you want to consider what has wiggle room and what you want to keep consistent. You have to think through the flexibility of it, or else it's not going to happen.
>
> —*Margaret Summers*

3. **Create visuals so students see and understand the routine's structure.** Visuals are helpful in reminding students what to do and why they are doing it. You can make visuals yourself or ask students to help create them (see *Sample Materials* at the end of the strategy). Visuals may include:
   - A list of steps that students need to take.
   - Sticky notes with students' names for groups.
   - A calendar.
   - Station directions.

4. **Introduce each routine using interactive modeling.** Show students how to do the steps, and then highlight best practices as students engage.
    - *Teacher Modeling:* Some examples of teacher modeling follow:
        - *Beginning:* "This is how I sit when I am taking mindful breathes (eyes closed, hands in lap, spine straight)."
        - *Middle:* "This is how I gather materials for my group (quietly, neatly in my basket, walking purposefully back to my table)."
        - *End:* "This is something that I want to remember for tomorrow's class because . . ."
    - *Highlight Student Thinking and Actions:* Some examples of highlighting students' thinking and actions include:
        - *Shout-outs:* "I like the way that _____ is sitting calmly."
        - *Freeze and Spotlight:* Tell students to freeze, and direct their attention at a student who is doing something well. "Look at how _____ put the supplies back."
        - *Responsiveness:* "What _____ shared was really important because . . ."

Be Intentional about Language

When introducing routines and developing visuals, be intentional about language. You are always using language, so you may as well be intentional about it. Think about the heart of what you are trying to do, and be sure your language reflects this.

---

5. **Implement the routine consistently.** Routines only become routine if they are practiced often! Remember that "practice makes progress!" A routine may not go as planned in the first few implementations. Have patience, adapt (if needed), and try again.

Every element that you've been taught rigidly about instruction doesn't matter if there's another way that will get you to the end goal in a better way.

—*Samantha Altman*

---

6. **Reflect individually and with students.** Think about how the routine facilitates thinking and learning and how it might be improved/adjusted. Consider:
    - *Impact:* Does the routine have the desired impact? (Think about your desired results.)
    - *Process:* Is the process working smoothly and efficiently for students?
    - *Evidence:* What products can you see or hear that result from the routine? (Are students focused? Did their reflections resonate with you and their classmates?) How does the classroom look? (Are supplies in place? Are students at their seats?)

STRATEGY IN ACTION: MAINTAINING AND EXTENDING ROUTINES

Buzz. "I got it!"

Buzzzzz . . . "No, I got it first!"

"It was me! I got it first! Look at what I built first!"

The Scene: Students with their laptops open aside a bag of change. An online buzzer system lights up on their faces. A game wheel sporting coin amounts flashes on the projector screen at the front of the room, spinning in a whirlwind of rainbow excitement. The teacher and paraprofessional circling the room checking answers as the buzzing rages on. A race to the finish—to build the change amount first.

The class ends with a single request, "Ms. A, can we play again tomorrow?"

This short scene is a narrative from my high school special education students enrolled in Consumer Math. Most of these students are planning to attend 18- to 21-year-old programs. Much of the content is the same day-to-day: It's about life skills and everyday examples. These students need repetition and routine to reinforce their learning, but that doesn't mean their experiences need to be dull or predictable.

We start each day with coin recognition skills practice. Students use coin identification sheets on which the first half is matching coins and the other side is color-coding. Though the routine remains consistent, certain aspects do change. I ask them, "What color do you want me to make this today?" Some students love choosing the color. This small variation makes the experience a bit fresher.

We know it is important for students to have multiple experiences with content, and I am all for adding and extending learning through games like the change-making challenge. Students can approach this with confidence because of the coin recognition routine.

If students are aware that they are scaffolding the same skill, it becomes dull, boring, and repetitive. Sometimes it becomes that way from initiation. Thinking creatively—marrying various methods, forms of engagement, and so on guarantees an enjoyable experience for all. When we enjoy learning, we remember, and maybe, just maybe, we don't even have to realize we're learning at all in the process.

—Samantha Altman

> ## WHY I LIKE THIS STRATEGY
>
> Being strategic and intentional with routines has allowed for deep learning in my classroom. Students know what to expect within a given routine, so as a class we can focus on everyone's thinking and ideas instead of going over ever-changing logistical information ("today you will need to go here") and directions.
>
> —*Margaret Summers*
>
> With special education students, routine is the name of the game. It's imperative when you walk in the room, you know what to do: get that laptop open, engage in procedures. After that first 15 minutes of routine and review, I don't necessarily want students to know what we are doing. They might know the goal, but the experience to get there can be more of a surprise if students have the initial benefit of routine to get them focused on learning.
>
> —*Samantha Altman*

Adaptation for Different Assets and Needs

Class Time	
Limited Time	*Lots of Time*
*Remember that routines can save you time. Establish a clear understanding of expectations and practice routines often so things run smoothly.	*Work with students to determine how to allocate your time based on their needs and preferences.
*Remember the importance of reflecting on actions and learning. Even a short reflection is valuable, so make sure to develop routines for reflection.	*Take time to discuss how elements of routines can extend into life outside of school (grounding, setting goals, acting purposefully, reflecting).

Teacher Personality	
Reserved/Strict	*Outgoing/Humorous*
*Develop structures for routines that make them work for your personality and leadership style.	*Integrate theatrical elements when creating and reinforcing routines.
*Assign student "routine monitors" to help with the logistics of the routines.	*Work into your plans ways to collaborate with students to highlight the fun and efficiency of classroom routines (e.g., use a stopwatch to show how quickly students cleaned up).

STRATEGY IN ACTION: PROBLEM-SOLVING WORKSHOP ROUTINE

One of my favorite routines in my classroom is called "Problem-Solving Workshop." The creation of this routine stemmed from multiple conversations with teachers at my school about a desire to rebrand math intervention to something more joyful, purposeful, and student-friendly. Problem-Solving Workshop was the name we decided to use for the 30 minutes of intervention time built into our math block.

When we came up with the new name, I figured it would be a good time to rethink my structure for this time block as well. I knew I wanted this time to be collaborative, meaningful, and fun. I wanted my students to really see themselves as problem solvers and look forward to this time every day.

I designed this block to start with a quick grounding conversation. Students gather in a circle and I introduce the topic ("We're thinking about fractions now.") and ask, "What's something you want to keep in mind?" Then we transition into intentionally designed groups that rotate each day. While students are working, I will ask about their process ("What do you do to find the least common denominator?" "How are you supporting each other?") and highlight student work ("I notice that this group is checking their work by . . ."). As we reach the end of the block, I turn off the lights to signal that it is time to clean up. Then we gather again and reflect as a community. Often students are eager to share. Sometimes I will prompt sharing by asking, "Did any group have someone do something really interesting?"

This routine sounds so simple, and I think any strong routine will seem that way. The magic really happens within the routine. The most complex and rich thinking has happened during this time. My students really look forward to this every day, and so do I!

—Margaret Summers

Chapter 4

Sample Materials

Daily Schedule

Problem Solving Workshop Group Assignments

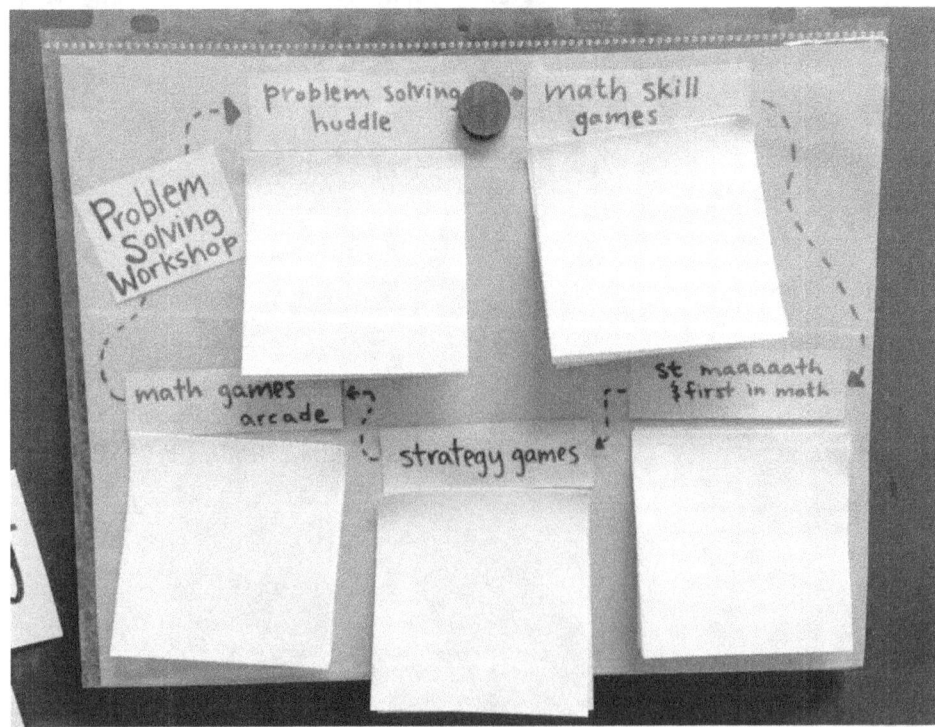

Planning for Instruction

STRATEGY 16: LESSON PACING

> Teacher Contributors
> *Hallie Brooks, P.S. 230 (NY), 2nd–3rd grades*
> *Heather Weck, Harriton High School (PA), 9th–12th grades*

Lesson pacing directly impacts student engagement and helps students explore the material in accessible bites while aiding them in making meaningful connections. Selecting the optimal order and style of activities, determining their length, and determining how they flow are all important in creating a classroom experience that helps students learn.

Strategy Implementation

1. **Determine the routines.** Come up with several routines that you will integrate into your classroom at the start of the year (see *Strategy 15: Incorporating Routines into Your Plans* and *Establishing Routines* in the first book in our series, *Adaptable Teaching: 30 Practical Strategies for All School Contexts*). Give each routine a code name so students have a common language to identify and execute the routine. These routines are parts of your lesson that students will do every day (or close to it). As you come up with each routine think about its:
   - *Timing:* Think about how long each routine will take each day. This will be critical to figuring out the flow of the lesson.
   - *Energy Level:* Figure out the level and type of energy needed to complete each routine. Is it a passive activity? A kinesthetic activity? Does it require talking or writing? You want to determine the energy level because it is important to mix up the energy levels of activities throughout the lesson to optimize flow and engagement.
   - *Collaboration:* Decide whether the routine is individual, pair, small group, or whole class. Note that if you have multiple routines, you will want to mix up the amount of collaboration students are doing for each of them so there is more variety in their experiences, which will impact the feeling and pace of students' learning.

> NOTE: Timing, energy level, and collaboration are elements—not just routines—to consider for every activity you plan in a lesson.

2. **Lesson parts and flow.** To determine the optimal flow and pacing to your lesson, consider the overall lesson time, timing for each activity, and of activities sequencing within the the lesson.
   - *Overall Lesson Time:* Based on how long your lesson is (45 minutes, 60 minutes, 90 minutes, etc.), you will need to think about how many activities you can include (along with your routine activities). Consider:

- *Timing for Each Activity:* The length of each activity should account for the age and attention span of your students, as well as:
    - *Manageable Chunks:* Any activity more than 15 minutes should be broken down and chunked into smaller parts so longer activities feel like a lot of manageable size activities that build on one another.
        - For instance, you can have a 40-minute activity that is broken into four parts that feel like four complementary activities rather than one very long 40-minute activity.
    - *Alternate Length:* Alternate longer and shorter activities so the lesson doesn't feel too much like rapid fire with lots of quick activities or drag on because of consecutive long activities. Also, remember the length is determined by:
        - *Difficulty:* The harder the topic, the longer the activity or activities.
        - *Importance:* The more important the topic is in relation to the day's or unit's goal(s), the more time you spend on it.
        - *Teacher- versus Student-Centered:* Ensure that more time is spent on student-centered work when possible. Remember that you are the facilitator and students learn best by *doing*.
    - *Build in Differentiation:* Differentiate based on student comfort and understanding of the material. Add in chunks and elements of lessons where additional supports and extensions are built in for any student who needs them. This keeps every student focused and engaged in an activity rather than finishing too early and getting restless or bored or not having enough time to finish an activity.

> Prioritize the most important parts of the lesson; the exploration and application should have the most weight/time. The application is where you see it start to click with your students.
>
> —Hallie Brooks

- *Sequencing Each Part of the Lesson:* Each lesson tells a great story with a strong beginning, middle, and end (see *Strategy 14: Story of Your Lesson(s)*).
    - *Beginning:* The beginning is typically a quick activity that hooks the students into and sets the stage for the rest of the lesson.
    - *Middle:* In the middle of the lesson, have at least two or more activities that help students learn and apply the content. The middle activities are ideally different lengths, alternating between longer and shorter, different energy levels, and different levels of collaboration.
    - *End:* Your ending activities help center students and bring them back to the goal(s) for the day.
        - NOTE: If you do not get to your concluding activity, make sure you take a few minutes to tie the activity your students are in the middle of at the end of class back to the goal(s) for the day.

> If you're consistent with the routine activities, it allows for you to have flexibility with the novel activities.
>
> —Heather Weck

3. **Variety and novelty.** As you plan activities to complement your routines, think about creating activities that feel new and novel to your students and that are different from one another. Keep in mind:
   - *Regularity:* Is the novel activity going to happen once or will it occur several times, like a mini-routine?

> Having things that students recognize (routines), it calms them, it calms me, and it can just get done without me talking a lot. Then that allows for more time to get into a novel activity. Also, I expect them to listen to those instructions and new information because the routines they are doing don't take that same type of brain power.
>
> —Heather Weck

   - *Variety:* Ensure the novel activities vary and engage students in different ways. Types of variety might include:
     - *Kinesthetic:* Plan an activity that gets students up and moving. It is important to ensure the instructions to the activity are explicit so students are clear on exactly what they are doing and why they are doing it when they are moving around the classroom.
     - *Artistic:* Let students get creative with your content. This could mean drawing, constructing, making videos, photography, and so on.
     - *Games:* Turn your activity into something competitive where students can play against one another. Design the games where they are inclusive of all students, taking into consideration: student temperaments; athleticism (if applicable); size of competitions; and something for everyone to do throughout the activity, even if they have been knocked out of the game.
     - *Stories:* Have students turn what they are learning into stories of some kind. The stories could be through pictures, words, videos, or any other medium that enables students to apply what they have been learning.
     - *Real World:* Design an activity that applies what students have been doing to their lived experiences. Create experiences where students see directly how what they have learned can and is used in the real world or how it can impact it.

> When students have fun, they remember the experience and then they can relate it to new experiences. You can do so much more when you're happy and excited about something.
>
> —Hallie Brooks

   - *Complementary:* As you design your novel activities, each one should complement the routine activities your students do daily. This will ensure the flow throughout the lesson and help with lesson placing. By creating routines *and* novel activities, you help students feel comfortable every day because they know what to expect (routines) while being kept "on their toes" by integrating different novel activities each day into the lesson. Having this balance between structure and surprises will create a more inclusive learning environment that engages students throughout the lesson.

Give Novel Activities a Few Tries

Novel activities sometimes need more than one chance to work. Students (and you) need time to see what works and adjust the process if needed. If a new activity doesn't go smoothly the first time, reflect with your students on how to make it work better next time.

---

4. **Assess the flow and pacing.** After designing the routine and novel activities, figure out how to best sequence the activities for both content and flow. When considering optimal flow, think about timing, energy level, and collaboration. You want to vary each of these so students stay energized, engaged, and curious.

5. **Make the pacing visible.** It is common practice to post the day's agenda for students. However, consider adding the pacing and flow to the agenda where students see the agenda more like an "itinerary" for a trip they are going on. This way, you introduce it at the start of class and then you look back at the day's itinerary with your students throughout the day to say, "this is what we are doing now and where we are going." Note that the timing may change as needed.

6. **Assess and reassess pacing.** After teaching a lesson or lessons, critically reflect on the flow and pacing. Ask yourself about:
   - *Timing:* If activities took too long or were too short, how can you better determine timing for activities?
   - *Engagement:* If students seem to get bored, how can you mix up the activities to retain engagement?
   - *Energy:* If students lose energy, how can you integrate more low-energy activities?

A SAMPLE STRUCTURE FOR LESSON PACING

I use a lesson planning structure called the Learning Cycles (Cavallo and Marek, 1997). It is a five-step lesson plan structure that differs greatly from the workshop model (I do, we do, you do), in that it has more exploration and discussion. The steps are **engage**, **explore**, **explain**, **apply**, and **assess**. Each step helps students construct their understanding of the content while still receiving explicit instruction. Each component has a specific amount of time.

Each component tells you exactly what it entails and a ratio of time.

Engage should be a brief hook to grab students attention, no more than 2–3 minutes. It can be a question, an image, or a game. You want to grab students' attention to get them excited with a hook that is related to the lesson and can be lots of fun.. Lengthy hooks can take away from what students need in the lesson. A quick hook helps with pacing and long-term engagement.

Then students **explore** this concept for about 10 minutes. This can be a tactile exploration, a discussion, or a group activity, but it is entirely student directed and independent from the teacher. You want it to be students grappling with the problem they need to solve and then explore how to figure it out. For instance, you might start by showing student work with errors to figure out how to correct it or have students figure out how to solve something or grapple with the content to understand the work they are doing.

Next is the **explanation** or debrief. This discussion can be 10–15 minutes and should be directed by students but facilitated and guided by the teacher to provide clarity. To make this debrief meaningful and engaging, you have to know your students. Pore over the questions you're going to ask ahead of time and the anticipated answers. Initially, when a novice, think about open-ended questions or offer choices for students (based on your students) to guide the discussion. Then integrate turn-and-talks; try to get students to talk to one another because they learn so much more from one another.

Then students **apply** newly acquired skills or knowledge with another hands-on activity for 10–15 minutes. It could be another exploration to build off of the previous one, applying the skill you just refined, and having a chance to build on the main takeaways from the explanation.

Finally, I **assess** students using quick data collection like a checklist, exit ticket, or brief closing discussion for 2–3 minutes. Note, you should be assessing during the application, so when you get to the conclusion assessment, you can pull out student work to highlight and provide relevant closure or do an exit ticket to collect.

The whole thing takes 45–50 minutes.

When things don't go as planned, there is some wiggle room to stretch a lesson or to have extension activities (problems/games). You may need to spend more time on explicit explanations if the exploration isn't working as planned or spend more time on exploration if it is really working.

—Hallie Brooks

> **STRATEGY IN ACTION: ROUTINES AND NOVEL ACTIVITIES IN CHEMISTRY CLASS**
>
> A routine I establish on Day 1 is the To-Do list. Students will certainly tell me if it's not up when they walk in the door. Having multiple bullet points allows students reentry points if they lose focus.
>
> A lesson outline for one day this winter included the following on our To-Do list:
>
> - Active warm-up [Novel]
> - How to use VSEPR reference sheet [Routine]
> - Model kit activity [neither]
> - Lewis structure mini-quiz 1 (top 2 out of 4 scores will count) [Novel, becomes a mini-routine]
>
> An active warm-up is used a couple of times a year. In this case, there are two categories: ionic and covalent bonding. Students come up with an action for each (e.g., marching in place, uppercuts, touching toes). I call out statements and students have to do the action that corresponds to the category.
>
> Although the concept of the VSEPR model is new to students, reference sheets have been established as a routine. They are copied to colorful paper and students know they will get access to them on assessments. Students generally listen up and are excited to add a new colored sheet to their collection.
>
> Mini-quizzes get used as novel activities just by switching up some aspects. For instance, you could tell students that the best two out of four scores count or give them a master list of possible questions and pick three out of a beaker each day. The point is to keep the stakes low but the hype high.
>
> The pacing for the day works because the active warm-up is silly and students enjoy it. They might not get a ton of content out of it, but it sets them up to take in information for the rest of the day. The trick is to not spend copious amounts of time on any one thing. With that said, you can't forgo directions because students will be confused and that will be a waste of time. The keys are going from one thing to another but never too quickly, giving instructions when you need to and having moments when you don't need to give instructions because they just know it. For some students, that's where the buy-in is, and for some students the buy-in is with the novel activities.
>
> This strategy is nothing mind-blowing, but it made for a good day of teaching with solid pacing and engagement for students (and very few students asked to go to the bathroom or had their phones out, and that's a win!).
>
> *—Heather Weck*

WHY I LIKE THIS STRATEGY

I like this strategy because it is explicit for me. It helps me plan for which components should take the most time in order to help the students do the thinking. They shouldn't be sitting staring at me for more than 10 minutes at a time; they should be interacting and moving. This is what I think about when planning those tasks. It's logical pacing; you get kids excited [and] have them build on excitement through exploration. Then give them a peek behind the curtain about what they just did. Then you have them do it again with that behind-the-scenes info and assess whether they understood it. Give them more, a little more, [and] then set them free! It creates more sustainability for the students; when kids have a chance to explore, everyone participates. Learning is loud, messy, and fun.

—Hallie Brooks

I focus on lesson pacing because it's easy to plan lessons when keeping this in mind. Additionally, it ensures that transitions are efficient for students; you can show them your "to-do" list to let them know what's coming next, giving them a heads up and reminders of what [you] are doing. Lastly, I focus on lesson pacing because two reasons students might check out are confusion and boredom. This strategy tows the line between familiarity and trying something new; it's rare that students will be both confused and bored. Routine helps eliminate confusion and can be a "win" for them because they always know what to do and how to do it, and novel activities help eliminate boredom. These activities, and the pacing that comes with them, provide students with on-ramps. You can lose focus at any point and with good pacing you have points where you can get back on track!

—Heather Weck

Adaptation for Different Assets and Needs

Class Time	
Limited Time	*Lots of Time*
*Limit the number of transitions, so students can stay engaged in what matters.	*Know your students and how many activities and transitions are feasible for them. Find the optimal balance between keeping students moving and engaged with doing too many activities.
*Have at least one main novel activity that changes in type from day to day.	
	*Focus on integrating multiple novel activities each day that are different from one another.

Planning Time	
Limited Time	*Lots of Time*
*You can use routine from one prep as a novelty for another prep.	*Reevaluate routines as the year goes on, adding in new routines with the help of student input.
*Do variations on novel activities that feel new to students, but are actually just an adaptation to a novel activity you have done with them before (e.g., changing a gallery walk that students do individually to a silent conversation between students where they write notes to each other about images placed around the classroom).	*Get creative and add unique novel activities for as many days as you can each week.

STRATEGY IN ACTION: PLANNING FOR PACING STARTS WHEN LEARNING TO TEACH

I learned how to use Learning Cycles to pace lessons in college at Syracuse University, but I didn't really start using it until I began writing my own curriculum. My first few years teaching were in charter schools where everything was planned and created for us. I was working in a fifth-grade Integrated Co-Teaching (ICT) math class as the special education teacher, and my general education teacher and I were looking for ways we could co-plan for small groups within the same lesson. We wanted our class to still feel like one community while also addressing the diverse needs our students had in math.

We used the Learning Cycles approach to pacing lessons (see "A Sample Structure for Lesson Pacing") and did the *engage* and *explore* as a whole class and would have the *application* as small groups. Depending on the lesson, the debrief (*explanation*) could be all together or in small groups. It worked very well and even though we didn't stay together as co-teachers the following year (she stayed in fifth grade and I moved down to third grade), we both kept using the strategy with our co-teachers. Some other colleagues used this template to inform their planning so that students were more engaged and on task since students need to change what they're doing periodically.

This really helped with pacing and, therefore, engagement. Our students were most impacted because they were able to do the work we set out for them to do. A big takeaway for me is that sometimes, the simplest solutions work best.

—*Hallie Brooks*

STRATEGY 17: CONNECTING SKILLS AND CONTENT WITH STUDENTS' LIVES AND INTERESTS

> Teacher Contributors
> Nita Luthria Row, Bombay International School (India), 5th grade
> Kimberly Radostits, Oregon Junior/Senior High School (IL), 8th –12th grades

Once you know your students' interests and backgrounds you can tailor your plans to ensure students find meaning in what you are teaching. This will enhance their learning and engagement in class. Knowing that your teaching plans should always reflect your students means that you go into each year with a framework for what and how you want to teach your material *and* that you are prepared to adapt plans to the needs, background, and interests of your students.

Strategy Implementation

Part I: General Planning Strategies for the Year, Units, and Lessons

1. **Make a general plan.** Before the school year starts and you get to know your students, map out your year based on what you know about your school's demographics and what you or your colleagues have taught in the past.
   - *Understand Your School's Demographics:* You can ascertain information about your school's student body, whether you have been there for years or are just starting out, by doing the following:
     ○ Look at data breaking down the school's demographics provided by the school or on the school website.
     ○ Talk to administrators, teachers, and/or parent coordinators to better grasp the cultural background of the students in the school; aim to understand deeper cultural elements of student populations at the school beyond superficial elements of the students. For instance:
       - In addition to learning about the languages and holidays cultural groups speak and celebrate, try to better grasp cultural communication styles and preferences and rituals that inform their daily lives.
     ○ Speak to the previous year's teacher(s) to learn about the backgrounds of your incoming students. Discussion might focus on topics such as students' preferred styles of communication, cultural or religious beliefs related to the curriculum you are teaching, or how students were made to feel included and when and where they felt excluded.
   - *Yearlong Overview/Calendar:* Based on the curriculum you need to teach and your basic understanding of the student populations at the school, map out your year's curriculum paying particular attention to creating goals and objectives that align with the school's students (see *Strategy 1: Yearlong Overview*).
   - *Unit Plans*: Although it does not make sense to plan out each unit for the year in great detail before meeting your students, plan out your first unit based on the more general demographic and cultural information you have learned about your incoming students. Think about ways you can use this unit as a way to get to

know your students. Then sketch out the remaining units for your year, leaving space for adapting your plans for new information you learn about your students once the year begins.
- *Lesson Plans:* Plan out the first week's lessons in detail based on the general demographic and cultural knowledge, and leave the remaining lessons in outline form to fill in relevant information after learning specific details about your new students.
- NOTE: If you have taught the course you are teaching in your school previously, use those plans as your baseline for the upcoming year, but note where in your yearlong overview/calendar and unit plans you will likely make changes once you get to know your students.

SAMPLE GETTING-TO-KNOW-YOU ACTIVITIES

Kimberly Radostits uses variations of the following activities to help her students get to know one another.

- **Grid Activities:** Students have to get up out of their chairs and find a peer that can relate to a characteristic described on a grid. For example, "Eats Turkey on Thanksgiving," "Has more than five people over for dinner on Sundays," and so on. (Grids can either be premade, or you can fill in some of the grid and leave boxes open for students to add details together before starting the activity.) Students are required to fill out their entire grid without repeating signatures. After students are done, bring it back together to have a student share about one thing that they had signed and then have other students talk about who did the similar thing. This builds community as students connect over sharing the same quality/indicator or they become curious about others with descriptors that do not match them. Continue to use the grid throughout the unit, selecting items many students identified with. For instance, select the information in each grid based on what you know about your students and local culture that is inclusive of your students. You can also use student responses from previously in the unit that helped you learn more about them.
- **All the Same/All Unique Activity:** Students get paired into three different groups. At their first group, they all tell something about themselves related to the subject of the day that they think they all share. For example, "I love pancakes with maple syrup" where they get as many members of their group as possible to agree. This is followed by a second group where they all try to say something about themselves that is unique to them like, "I eat honey on my toast." This is an activity that will help plan future activities.
- **Student Generated Gallery Walk:** Have students describe their culture(s) by writing down locations, customs, practices, and so on. Then after gathering the students' perspectives and information about their cultures, add additional facts that the students might have left out that can help deepen students' understanding and provide a more holistic perspective of different cultures. Next, put each separate culture on its own paper/chart that you then hang around the room. Finally, have students walk around the room to learn about each other's cultures in the class, taking note of similarities and differences between their cultures.

2. **Get to know your students. There are several ways to get to know your students. Try one of the following:**
   - *Student Interest Forms:* On the first or second day of school, give your students an interest form with questions about what they like most, dislike, enjoy doing at home and school, and other information you want to know about your students. This can be done using Google Forms, on paper, through pictures or images, or any way that is accessible to all of your students.
   - *Getting-to-Know-You Games:* During the first week of school, plan at least one getting-to-know-you game each day where you and the students learn more about one another. Each of these games should be designed so every student feels comfortable as possible and is engaged in getting to know everyone. There should be a mixture of more superficial icebreakers where you and your students learn general facts about each other, and some games that challenge everyone to learn about what makes them tick. For instance:
     - *Superficial Things to Learn:* Interests, skills, talents, hobbies, etc.
     - *Deeper Qualities:* Values, important connections with others, etc.
   - *Talk to Your Students:* Whenever you get the chance, before, during, or after class, talk to your students to learn more about them. This might be chatting with students between classes or as they enter your room, having one-on-one conferences with them where you talk to them about more than your curriculum, or going to their after-school activities to see them doing what they love.
   - NOTE: Read the second book in our series, *Creating Positive Classroom Climate: 30 Practical Strategies for All School Contexts* Strategies 7 and 8, to learn more about getting to know your students.

3. **Adapt your general plans. When thinking about how best to meet student where they are, consider the following:**
   - *End Goals:* Examine your end goals for the year and your units to determine whether the goals will work with what you learned about your students or whether you need to tweak each goal to better align with who your students are. (For more on determining learning goals, see *Strategy 6: Determining Learning Goals*.)
   - *Curriculum:* Take what you have learned about your students and revisit your curriculum–texts, assessments, and projects. Look for ways the curriculum can directly reflect the interests and background of your students. This includes adopting texts where students can see themselves and learn about one another and projects and other assessments that have real meaning to the students.
   - *Skills:* Getting to know your students includes understanding the skills that students already possess and where they need to grow. To do this, think about the skills you want to help your students build throughout the year and integrate short activities at the start of the year to assess students' levels with each skill. Once you have learned this:
     - Scaffold your activities to support the needs of each of your students.
     - Adapt your pedagogical approach to meet your students where they are while supporting and challenging each student to meet your end goals.

- For instance, if a large number of students said that they found it difficult to focus on reading or to find topics to write about, conduct mini-lessons to support their reading focus and brainstorm writing ideas together. In case only a few students needed help with certain aspects of reading and writing, support them during one-on-one conferences with them.

> Connecting the skill and content with students' lives and interests helps students feel that "my teacher cares" from the very beginning of the year. It's nice to know that your teachers don't just view you as the next batch/cohort of students. I'm interested in you and want to get to know you, and I care. Starting off on that note gives students this feeling that they count and are valued.
>
> —*Nita Luthria Row*

4. **Give students a say.** Build in opportunities for your students to have a say in your curricular plans, including assessments, texts, and projects that align with their interests, skills, and talents. This might include sharing a list of texts for an upcoming unit with your students and asking them to point out narratives or perspectives that are missing or offer choices for assessments where students have the option to design their own assessment that meets particular criteria and goals.

5. **Reevaluate.** As often as you can (on-the-spot, daily, weekly, monthly), reevaluate your plans based on what you continue to learn about your students. Then tweak your plans as needed, even if the entire plan needs to change to align better with your students' interests and needs.

> It's not building the plane as you fly it, but when you feel you need to tweak, you do it. . . . it's a highly responsive model of teaching. If you need to spend more time because they're not getting it, or you need to spend less time because they're not interested, or it's not working, or they don't need it when previous cohorts did, you scrap it . . . see how things are going then decide.
>
> —*Nita Luthria Row*

Part II: Planning Strategies for Parts of a Lesson

1. **Beginning of the lesson.** It is ideal to start each class by helping students see themselves reflected in the content. This allows every student an opportunity to feel like they belong while completing an exercise that feels relevant; this sets the stage for students to remain engaged throughout class. To plan such activities:
   - *Offer Choice and Flexibility:* When designing a prompt, ensure students have freedom to come up with an answer that is meaningful to them; therefore, the prompt must be something that is written with multiple possible answers or options for how to answer it.
   - *Design Prompts to Reflect on Student Experiences:* Think about the content and skills you are teaching for the day. Then consider what you know about your

students and come up with a prompt that enables each student to reflect on their own relationship or experiences related to the content for the day. You want to ensure the prompt is inclusive of all of your students; so, if some of your students are really into sports, you could create a prompt about "competition" rather than focusing specifically on sports, as all students experience competition in some aspect of their lives.
- ○ For example, in Kimberly Radostits' Spanish classroom, during a food unit, she had her students list their favorite foods, reflect on meaningful meals they have eaten, or write about customs their family has during mealtimes. That information was then used to connect to class content for the period.

> Giving your students that small opportunity to have a success at the start of the lesson is so critical. It makes every student feel they belong in the room because they all have a story to share, regardless of how much they know the content.
>
> —*Kimberly Radostits*

2. **Middle of the lesson.** The middle of your lesson should integrate different ways for students to feel connected to what they are learning. Some types of activities to plan include:
   - *Think-Pair-Shares:* Integrate as many think-pair-shares as you can throughout the middle part of the lesson because this is a space where students, with explicit prompts, can connect in intimate settings with peers about the content.
   - *Photo/Video Prompts:* Photo or video prompts allow students to reflect on their experiences and share in think-pair-share scenarios and are accessible to all students regardless of skill set. When selecting and planning activities around photos or videos:
     - ○ Consider the background of your students and if any photos or videos might be triggering (e.g., a photo of a grandparent and grandchild after a student recently lost a grandparent).
     - ○ Be intentional about selecting things that bring certain vibes and emotions to the classroom. For instance, if you want to have a more vibrant conversation, choose something that has shock value. If you want to make it personal, choose something they can connect with based on what you know about your students.

> **Using Photos of Student Experiences in Presentations**
>
> In my class, a disengaged student joined a local hockey team and he'd been quiet about it, but shared it in a bell-ringer. I then followed up with him about his hockey, then went to go watch a match and took pictures. When we were in the classroom, I projected the pictures on our screen and talked about the match. Then I asked the student to talk about it. This student went from reserved to someone who was excited to share his experiences with hockey, and other students started to see him in a different way. This experience was a springboard to learn about students' other passions in out-of-school-sponsored activities.
>
> —*Kimberly Radostits*

- Think about the emotions and analysis from the video or photo that you can integrate into the rest of your lesson.
- *Presentations:* Teacher and student presentations are a great way to demonstrate how students are connected to your class material. There are subtle differences in how teachers and students prepare presentations presentations:
  - *Teacher:* When preparing a presentation to give your students, be intentional about images and videos you integrate into your presentation while also adding slides that make explicit and direct connections between what students are learning and their backgrounds. You can also consider adding slides that ask students to make their own connections to the material.
  - *Student:* When you have students create their own presentations, require that they include slides that make direct links to the content as well as adding analysis of why and how they included images and text based on their unique perspectives. You should also give students choice in how they present their work so they can express themselves in ways they are interested in and comfortable (e.g., slide deck, song, poem, photo essay).
- *Student-Centered Learning:* If you make your classroom more student-centered where you serve as a facilitator and students are engaged in collaborative learning, it will allow you to float around the room and learn more about your students, which is information you can integrate into future lessons. It is much more difficult to connect with students when the class is lecture-heavy.

3. **End of the lesson. The end of the lesson is a time to solidify the content and skills you explored together. To do this:**
   - *Examine Impact:* Have your students explore how the content and skills they learned throughout the lesson will impact their lives and community.
   - *Circle Back:* If you created a beginning of class activity that connects to students' lives, come back to that connection with an exit ticket or short exercise that challenges students to make deeper connections to the material based on what they learned throughout the lesson.

STRATEGY IN ACTION: MAKING MEANING OUT OF PHOTOS

Every year my students do a unit on food and the cultural perspective of mealtimes in the Spanish speaking world. As an intro to that unit, I project a photo of a group of people sharing a meal in their home. I ask students to think-pair-share with their peers on who is in the photo, what they are eating, when the meal is taking place and to make some predictions on why the group is gathered.

Often students will tell me that they think it must be a special event because there appears to be an extended family all together and that it must be taking place for dinner because of the types of food. After having that discussion, I usually ask students to share one fact about themselves and mealtimes that they think *all* students would have in common and one fact about themselves and mealtimes that they believe is unique to them.

Last year, I had several students in my class that were often disengaged in school and would choose not to participate. With this activity, in particular, these students all were willing to share their voice and make connections because it was something they had ownership of and could be confident about. The quietest of them all said to me "I thought it would be easier to find something that was different about me. What I realized through doing this is that we are all a lot more similar than I thought." That comment has stuck with me because building community in a class and/or building is extremely important for student success.

Allowing students to discover that they *did* have a lot in common with each other *and* the content we were discussing made it so that they were a lot more focused on what we were working on—and they scored higher on that exam than most others. The overall outcome of this activity is that my students realized they weren't really different from others in the room, including for the students who had been more marginalized than others who had been more successful in school up to that point.

My first time doing this years ago, I asked the question about who eats with their parents, and the only two students who did not raise their hands were really embarrassed. I learned it is important to let students decide what they want to share and how they share. Once I realized this, students were willing to decide what parts of themselves they wanted to share, whereas previously I had unintentionally outed students I didn't mean to. Therefore, I am now intentional about students being able to share what they are comfortable with.

—*Kimberly Radostits*

WHY I LIKE THIS STRATEGY

If students feel valued, connected to the content, and have a say in things, then they are not just being taught but are learning themselves; they end up feeling more motivated. When they are not passive recipients and can exercise choice where their voices are valued, they will be far more engaged.

—*Nita Luthria Row*

John Keller's ARCS model (2010) of motivation states that humans are motivated toward tasks that include one of four elements: Attention, Relevance, Confidence, and Satisfaction. Empowering student voice hits all four elements in that it is directly relevant to a students' lives, catches their attention by learning from their peers, helps them develop confidence in that they can already have baseline knowledge from their own lives that they can use to acquire new knowledge through connections, and brings them satisfaction in learning from each other. It's a mindset going into each lesson; it means when delivering the lesson, adjust if your intent is not being met and then come up with something else that does motivate your students (either in the moment or before the next lesson). I ensure that I keep ARCS in mind as I plan and through reflection and adaptations that I make to lessons.

—*Kimberly Radostits*

Adaptation for Different Assets and Needs

Curricular Freedom	
Limited Freedom	*Lots of Freedom*
*Do the activities that are required more efficiently to allow time for other activities that are more catered to the needs of your students. Most districts won't say you can't add curriculum, you just can't take away. *Adding photos and videos and getting-to-know-you games beyond the required curricula can greatly enhance students' connections to the content and skills you are teaching.	*Ensure that a significant percentage of your unit and lesson end goals relate to students' lives and interests. *Integrate connections, where possible, into the beginning, middle, and end of your lessons.

Cultural Diversity	
Limited Diversity	*Lots of Diversity*
*Intentionally integrate new cultures into your curriculum in a way that students can see how their own culture and backgrounds are similar and different. (See *Strategy 5: Culturally Responsive/ Sustaining Teaching*.) *Ensure you honor the diversity you have in the classroom in a way that respects how the student(s) want to be included without "othering" them and putting them on the spot to be the token diversity student.	*Explicitly integrate and lift up all of the cultures and voices within the classroom as much as possible. *Provide space for students to connect their own cultures to what they are learning.

STRATEGY 18: INTENTIONAL GROUPINGS AND DESIGNING GROUP WORK

> Teacher Contributors
> *Alisa Ettienne, Asociación Escuelas Lincoln (Argentina), 6th–8th grades*
> *Michelle Zimmerman, Renton Prep (WA), 7th–10th grades*

When planning group work, it is important to create intentional groupings that both challenge students and allow them to succeed. Intentional groupings are strategically created with explicit and concrete instructions that ensure all students are engaged and participating. Such groupings also help individual students learn valuable academic, social, and practical skills that they will use inside and outside the classroom.

Strategy Implementation

Part I: Intentional Groupings

1. **Time of the year.** How you plan your groups will shift based on the time of year and your knowledge and understanding of your students. Consider:
   - *Start of the Year:* Groupings at the start of the year are formed to get a sense of your students and what optimal groupings throughout the year might look like. Think about:
     - *Random Groups:* Putting students in random groups to get a feel for what students are like, how they interact, who sticks together and who is isolated, who takes on different roles, their personalities, their perspectives/viewpoints, and general group dynamics.
     - *Getting-to-Know You Elements:* Integrating getting-to-know-you elements into each group activity during the first week so students get to know each other and you get to know each of them. To have a community, you must know each other; therefore, find things to bond over.
     - *Varied Perspectives:* Focusing on challenging students to take and explore multiple viewpoints. This will help you see stances they take, how they engage with one another, and how they need support in navigating dialogue with varied perspectives or opening up to other perspectives if only one viewpoint dominates the group.
   - *Once You Know Your Students:* After getting to know your students, you can intentionally form groups based on what you have learned about your students and their dynamics. This includes interests, friend groups, abilities, talents, knowledge demonstrated, and so much more.

2. **Determining group makeup.** Once you know your students and their assets and needs well, it is important to consider multiple factors when determining the makeup of groups.
   - *Content Knowledge:* Students have varying levels of understanding related to what they are learning. When creating groups, think about whether it is best

to group students who have similar levels of knowledge or various levels of knowledge.
- ◦ *Various Levels of Knowledge:* If you are grouping students heterogeneously, be strategic in putting students together who will support one another in other ways (personality, roles, interests, skills, etc.) and where the student(s) with greater knowledge will be willing and able to support the students who struggle more. You want to avoid a situation where the student(s) who understand the material better dominate the work or feel obligated to do it all; rather, you want the groups to work as a cohesive team that compliments their different strengths.
- ◦ *Similar Knowledge:* Grouping students homogeneously allows you to push the students who understand the material well already and build in supports for students who are struggling with the material. If you choose to group students this way, ensure that it is done in a way where students who struggle are not made to feel inferior to the students who grasp the material better. To avoid this situation:
  - Create a classroom environment early in the year where students understand that they all have different strengths and areas of growth and that they will be grouped in "strength" and "areas of growth" groups from time to time.
  - Make the groupings *appear* random, when in fact you are putting students together who have similar levels of knowledge (e.g., you can do this by counting off, but paying close attention to who is getting what number so certain students are grouped together or separated).
- *Skills:* Try to balance groups so each group has students with varying and complementary skills and abilities. This will allow each student a chance to shine as well as for students to learn from one another. It might be difficult to find the optimal balance of skills between students; therefore, consider the roles you want students to take on during the group work and assign students to groups with those roles and their varying skills in mind.
- *Personality:* Most classes are full of students with diverse personalities, from talkative to quiet, outgoing to shy, funny to serious, and so on. Be cognizant of how you mix up those personalities when putting groups together. For instance, you could put one talkative student in each group to generate a discussion. Which personalities you put in each group will be based on what you're looking for in terms of group dynamics.
- *Interests:* To get optimal buy-in from groups, it can be helpful to group students who share similar interests that align with what they are working on as a group, helping them to come together organically toward achieving their common goal(s). Conversely, you might want to group students with varying interests that align with the different roles they need to take on within their group.
- *Motivation:* Motivation is a critical part of any group work, where highly motivated students often dominate the work and less motivated students take a step back to let the motivated students do the work. To account for this, consider

grouping students based on motivation level. (See Strategy in Action: Using Motivation (and Not Skill or Knowledge) to Group Students.)
- *Friendships:* Students typically want to work with their friends, which can be useful or distracting depending on the dynamic. To accommodate students' desire to work with friends while also accounting for optimal group dynamics you hope to manage, have students make a list of students they want to work with as well as one or two students they do *not* think they can effectively work with. Then promise them you will put them with at least one person they want to work with and that you won't put them with the individual(s) they noted. Students will feel a sense of ownership over the group selection and will be less likely to complain about the overall groupings because they had a say in the selection.
- *Teacher versus Student Selection:* There are times where it makes sense for students to select their own groups and you just support their needs. When this is the case, decide the size of the group and any necessary roles. Then when students select their own groups set the expectation that they will:
  - Have a culture of inclusiveness where students actively seek out students who do not have a group rather than having students without a group feeling like nobody wants them.
    - This is something that must be built into your classroom culture early in the year and practiced consistently. Students must know that if inclusiveness is not achieved, students will no longer have the opportunity to select their own groups.
  - Demonstrate clear intentionality in how they selected their groups to balance skills and choose people they normally don't interact with on a social level at school. (Note that there are times where students might want to just select groups with their friends, which is OK from time to time. If this is the case, they must still be inclusive as described previously.)
- *Random versus Intentional:* Although it often makes sense to intentionally group students, there are times where random group assignments are preferred. Random groups are often helpful when you are trying to evaluate your students in terms of knowledge or skills. If students are grouped randomly, you are more likely to see who takes on what roles and who seems to need more or less support.
- *Size:* Create groups that are big enough for effective student collaboration but not too big where students are unable to retain focus and engagement. The younger the students, the smaller the "largest" group size should be. In terms of optimal size:
  - *Elementary Students:* Form groups of three to four to give students ample opportunity to interact and contribute.
  - *Middle and High School Students:* Form groups of three to six students. If you have more than five or six students, even with clearly defined roles, it becomes difficult for the groups to self-regulate and stay engaged throughout the duration of their work.

STRATEGY IN ACTION: USING MOTIVATION (AND NOT SKILL OR KNOWLEDGE) TO GROUP STUDENTS

Motivation theory (Ryan & Deci, 2000) discusses intrinsic versus extrinsic motivation and the elements needed to help people persist when things get challenging. They identify what they call three innate psychological needs: relatedness, autonomy, and competence. When these three psychological needs are met, adults and children across cultures and different settings are more likely to persist when things get hard. This is why it's important to consider grouping students based on motivation.

Although it might seem counterproductive, I have found that it works well to group highly motivated students regardless of their skill level and group unmotivated students regardless of their skill level. In this scenario, motivated students get a chance to experience how dynamic learning can be when they all pull their weight and delve into learning the areas they need to learn to succeed. For students who hated group projects before because they were always with unmotivated students, many express the joy of collaborative work and how they never knew it could be fun and make them feel even more successful.

For unmotivated students who are used to relying on motivated people to do all the work, there may be an initial panic when they realize they are paired with fellow unmotivated students (even if they are highly skilled). When you see the panic set in, you can ask them to describe what they are thinking or feeling.

"It's not fair" will often come out.

You can ask, "what's not fair?"

"The good students are all together, and what am I supposed to do?" (or some version of this).

This is the fun part: "You are a good student. You get a chance to show your skills and brilliance and take the lead."

"But I don't want to do the work!"

"Oh. So are you saying that you wanted to be with that group because they do the work and you don't have to? See, I care about you so much, I want you to learn how to use your skills to accomplish things and not just rely on someone else. If I let you choose not to develop your skills, I wouldn't be a very effective teacher. I'm giving you a challenge now while I'm here to support you so that life will feel easier later when I'm not there to support you, and when you don't have someone to step in and do the work for you."

"But, but, none of us in this group do work. Everyone knows that!"

"Well, that's a decision you all make together. If none of you do anything, there will be nothing to submit and you won't be able to demonstrate your learning. If you don't demonstrate your learning, there won't be anything to score. Nothing to score means I can't put in a grade. But that will be your choice individually and as a team. Or, you can all decide together to show what I know you're capable of."

Sometimes, you see improvements immediately in effort. Sometimes it takes the shock value of not submitting anything. And in the cases where there are repeated decisions to not submit anything, it sends a message that there won't always be someone to pick up the pieces for them, so students realize the need for working together (relatedness), autonomy (self-motivation), and accomplishing tasks (competence).

—*Michelle Zimmerman*

INTENTIONALLY ASSIGN ROLES OR LET STUDENTS DECIDE?

Ideally, you will want to mix up intentionally assigning roles within groups and letting students choose their own roles. When doing both, consider:

- **Intentionally Assign Roles Based on Strengths:** Intentionally assign roles to students for a project based on their strengths and tell them why. Sometimes this surprises students. It does several things: (1) It lets them and the class or classmates in the group hear you commend a skill you see in a student (it may be the first time someone has verbalized that strength in a student and they may not be aware of that strength themselves, and hearing it from you can give them confidence as well as make others around them aware); (2) It can help model for students that drawing on different strengths can support forward momentum of a project so when they start designing and choosing groups sometimes, they have at least one skill they can articulate and say why they are forming teams (rather than just "uh because we're friends"); and (3) It focuses you as a teacher to look for positives in all students and keep note of that to find ways to support them and for the next type of intentional grouping.
- **Intentionally Assign Roles with Growth in Mind:** If the best way to learn is to *do*, then it makes sense to provide students with opportunities to develop their knowledge and skills through the roles they take on in group work. This may mean scaffolding what they need to do or assigning more than one student to a role so they have each other for support.
- **Let Students Decide Roles:** When letting students decide, you can either let them advocate for doing a role that highlights their strength(s) or challenges them to select a role that is an area of growth for them. Be explicit about what type of role you are asking them to take on (and that you will know if they just select a role that comes easily to them if you are asking them to select one that challenges them). You can also tell students to randomly assign roles that were different from their strength in the last project. Making it random will make it feel less threatening because all students are having to take on and learn new skills at the same time.

—*Michelle Zimmerman*

3. **Group roles and dynamics.** After determining the optimal group makeup, it is important to think about roles and dynamics within the group. Regardless of these roles and dynamics, first and foremost, you must ensure that each student has something to do at all times during the group work process (including the presenter if there is one) and that the work is equitable in terms of effort and time, even if the tasks are quite different (e.g., if a student is assigned a presenter or timekeeper role, that student would still be responsible for processes related to the K/S/D/ of the activity). Next, consider multiple elements to help the groups run as smoothly as possible:
   - *Roles:* During most group work, it is helpful to have students take on roles that give them specific tasks to work on as they work collectively toward the group's goal(s). Two roles that exist in most groups are *facilitator* to ensure that every group member is involved and has their voice heard and *timekeeper* to help the group pace their work. Other roles will depend on the type of group work and tasks, but might include roles such as researcher, writer, artist, or presenter (which should be accompanied with other tasks to get done). When designing group roles, consider:
     ○ *Challenge:* Ensure that every student is challenged within their given role to help them grow in terms of their readiness or abilities.
     ○ *Variety:* Change who takes on each role to push students who don't typically take on those responsibilities.
     ○ *Pushing Students out of Their Comfort Zone:* In addition to creating groupings that account for what students possess, consider groupings where students are pushed to develop skills, knowledge, and other traits that they don't possess or struggle with.
       - *Voices/Perspectives:* Create groups that include multiple voices and perspectives, and create protocols that allow for each of those voices to be heard. If you cannot create groups with authentically diverse voices and perspectives, build in elements into the work students are doing that challenge students to learn about and take on those new perspectives.

Ira Shor, analyzing Paulo Freire's critical pedagogy, argued that "classrooms die as intellectual centers when they become delivery systems for lifeless bodies of knowledge" (Shor, 1993). With group work, students have to participate and not just listen to *lifeless knowledge* as they, as a group, work to deepen and demonstrate the knowledge that they have acquired.

—*Alisa Ettienne*

   - *Accountability:* For groups to function optimally, they must hold each other accountable for the work they are doing—a sort of internal checks and balances. To do this, the group facilitator can check in with each member in terms of their work and progress, or group members can have their own checkpoints and then accountability partners within the group to help keep each other on track. (See "Group Work Progress Tracker" in *Sample Materials*.)

- *Identifying Failures and Redesigns:* Identifying what is not working within a group is important for individuals and groups to grow and learn from their mistakes. Therefore, begin by modeling how to make your thinking visible, identifying your own failures and how you redesigned from there. (For more on how to help students "Fail Forward," see the first book in our series, *Adaptable Teaching: 30 Practical Strategies for All School Contexts*.) When designing the groups and group work, build in checkpoints where groups need to identify what is not working, and then collaboratively work together to figure out how to redesign their tasks to work more effectively.
- *Feedback Processes:* Give each group feedback that provides encouragement and commends bravery, authenticity, transparency, and process over their final product.

Part II: Designing Group Work

1. **Selecting content and products.** Intentional groupings are often only as effective as the content, tasks, and products you are asking students to work with and create. Therefore, it is essential to strategically select content and design products that engage students and their groups. To do this, the content and products should focus on:
    - *Authentic Scenarios:* Design tasks and products that are based on authentic scenarios students may encounter in the real world. Then carefully select content that is meaningful and accessible to your students that will help them create a product that is relevant to their lives.
    - *Real-World Inquiry-Based:* Beyond making group work authentic, present it in a way that is inquiry-based. This way, the group must work together to uncover and solve problems; this will simulate real-world complexities that have no easy, known solution already in existence. Because this type of inquiry-based work can be challenging and frustrating to students:
        - *Provide Examples:* Give examples of times you have needed to develop the skills to solve problems and then have students share examples of times they have seen others need those skills.
        - *Multiple Possible Answers:* Let students know that you are not searching for one correct answer but, rather, to identify and present something unique and unexpected.
            - For instance, Michelle Zimmerman helps her students to identify and present something "unexpected" and will go through some simple exercises to establish what she means by unexpected rather than "expected" responses. You can see step-by-step examples of how she started an approach to model Design Thinking in *Teaching AI: Exploring New Frontiers for Learning* (Zimmerman, 2018) and in *Complete the Line 2020* at https://wakelet.com/wake/st1NzJILdYH0ozYOHGlAS
    - *Student Choice:* There are multiple ways you can build student choice into group work. These include:

- *Offer Multiple Product Options:* Provide options for possible products students can produce in their groups. Then have students vote for a product they want to create and have them justify why they selected the product they chose.
- *Student Designed Product:* Offer students the chance to propose their own product based on the goal(s) of the group work or project. For their product to be approved, students must:
  - Defend how their product meets all the outcomes and goal(s) for the project.
  - Be persuasive about how their product is supported by evidence, considers their anticipated audience, and fits within a realistic time frame you established for the project.
  - Be prepared to create a draft of the product for peer and teacher review and feedback before revisions are made to the final product.

2. **Design the process and instructions.** For your intentional groupings to work effectively and efficiently, it is important to carefully construct the process and instructions for the group. Keep in mind:
   - *Clear Instructions:* With your product and end goal(s) or outcome(s) in mind, develop steps for your students to successfully complete the product. Your instructions should be broken down into clear steps in accessible language. If you are having trouble coming up with the optimal language, think about questions students might have about the process, and integrate your answers to those questions into your instructions. When breaking down your instructions remember to:
     - *Chunk:* To make the work accessible, break the tasks down into achievable pieces that are a reasonable amount of time for your age group (ranging from 5 to 15 minutes). Explicitly label the timing for each part of each task.
     - *Scaffold:* Think about the best ways to support each part of the process to make the tasks accessible for each of your students. Some students will need more support than others, so consider providing checklists for steps that need to be taken or templates/graphic organizers to help students ensure that they are on the right path.
   - *Check-In Questions:* Build in questions that students must answer at different points throughout their group work to determine how they are doing and what they have learned. This can be done formally where they must record answers and report back to you and their peers, or it could be done informally where they briefly discuss the answers with their group members and then move on. These questions can focus on tracking what they have learned, but also highlight areas where individuals and the entire group are struggling so they can evaluate how to grow from their struggles.
   - *Explicit versus Loose Instructions:* Explicit instructions are helpful to ensure students understand what to do and how to do it. However, as students get older, they need to develop skills for problem-solving and group work in spaces where every step is not laid out for them. This "gradual release" of moving from

explicit instructions to more general instructions can help students and groups build real-world problem-solving and autonomy skills.
- For instance, in some cases in life, there may be step-by-step instructions like putting together furniture or recipes for cooking and baking. But so many aspects of people's lives include being in situations with no known solution, and they need to determine their path to an end goal using the skills and tools they have.

- *Delivering Instructions:* You want to ensure all students clearly understand instructions for the group work before they begin. To do this, plan to give instructions before students move, and then reinforce them once students are in their groups; or have students move before going over instructions, and once everyone is settled in their groups, go over the instructions. Determine a way to have the instructions visible to the students (on the board or in front of them on paper/computer screen), read over them with the students (step-by-step), and have students ask questions and reinforce what they are doing before they begin working.

WHY I LIKE THIS STRATEGY

I like using intentional groupings because I am a keen believer in allowing students to learn through discovery and for students to have more initiative and to play a key role in the classroom. Classrooms tend to be hierarchical where the teacher is usually the main figure who guides the class and the students listen and then complete the task.

With intentional grouping, the students are key actors. When asked about how they would go about doing the task or ideas that could help them successfully execute the task, they often refer to different styles and methods of learning such as visual, auditory, kinesthetic, etc.

—*Alisa Ettienne*

I like using intentional groupings because it helps students to articulate their story in their voice for an audience who wasn't part of the experience. Students get to be creative communicators, focus on the learning process over a letter grade, and experience how to collaborate as part of a team. Through group work, students and their teams are able to articulate their process, failures, redesigns, and ultimately the standards (outcomes/goals) that they met.

—*Michelle Zimmerman*

Adaptation for Different Assets and Needs

Class Size	
Small Class	*Large Class*
*Plan to vary the mix of students in groups frequently so students get a chance to work with different peers.	*Plan to use the same groupings multiple times so students get a chance to form relationships and establish small group dynamics.
*Designate areas in the classroom for each group to create their own working space.	*Arrange for groups to work in the hallway or the library if they need a quiet place rather than the large crowd.

Academic Diversity	
Limited Diversity	*Lots of Diversity*
*Focus on creating grouping based on a diversity of personality, demographic, and personality traits.	*Check in with individual group members to determine how confident they are contributing to the work and how they are supporting their peers.
*Design roles that explicitly challenge students to grow and rotate roles consistently throughout the year.	*Vary the way you form groups. Create mixed ability groups for some activities, and for others, use ability-based grouping. (See *Strategy in Action: Using Motivation (and Not Skill or Knowledge) to Group Students*.)

STRATEGY IN ACTION: USING KNOWLEDGE OF YOUR CLASS TO DESIGN GROUP INSTRUCTION

I taught a Grade 8 English Language Arts class in which students engaged in critical analysis of a novel. The aim of the lesson was for students to understand what indirect and direct characterization was and to notice where it was used in the novel.

To help the students think about direct and indirect characterization, I asked the students to come up with three positive adjectives to describe each of their peers in their small groups. I used this group-based instruction as I knew the students well, and I knew that they were quite social; they liked to discuss ideas and concepts, and they liked to demonstrate what they know.

While they described their peers, they were able to use initiative and show the vocabulary they knew and perhaps rediscover their familiarity with linguistic devices. For example, they could use alliteration so if their peer's name started with a particular letter they could find an adjective with that same letter. The students were using direct characterization. I then asked them why they described their peers that way in order for them to see an example of indirect characterization; an example: They are kind because I always see them including others.

The students enjoyed the strategy and it was special and memorable for them as it also allowed them to be mindful of others and to bond with their peers whilst learning. The small group element of this experience was important because it allowed for deeper personalization and connection among students. I believe that the students were the most impacted because, as well as learning, we shared a nice and positive experience. The big takeaway for me was that getting to know my students well helped me to deliver an effective and unforgettable lesson.

—*Alisa Ettienne*

Sample Materials

Group Work Progress Tracker

Name:
Date:
Group Members:
Project Title:

PART I – Plan for the Day

DIRECTIONS: Before diving into your group work, set a goal for the day. Discuss what you want to accomplish and how each group member can contribute.

Goal for the day:

Group Member Roles and Responsibilities:

PART II – Reflection

DIRECTIONS: Respond to the following questions to help you think about what you accomplished and what you need to do next.

How did you make progress toward this goal?

What did you individually contribute?

How well did your group collaborate? Explain.

What do you think you and your group need to do next?

STRATEGY 19: CONSIDERING EQUITY AND MULTIPLE PERSPECTIVES

> Teacher Contributors
> *Akiko Mazor, P.S. 230 (NY), Kindergarten*
> *Rachel Scupp-Jorge, Thomas R. Grover Middle School (NJ), 8th grade*

Considering equity and multiple perspectives while planning is important for creating an inclusive classroom learning environment. Equity and multiple perspectives should be at the core of all planning decisions in both explicit and implicit ways; this includes overt curricular decisions and being intentionally aware of the hidden curriculum that exists in your school and classroom. Hidden curriculum includes what is not explicitly taught to students, (e.g., a social expectation like how to behave in classroom competitions) or conveying societal norms and values that sometimes reinforce biases (e.g., only asking boys to carry materials in the classroom). Considering equity and multiple perspectives can take many forms in planning, including how the curriculum is framed, texts selected, assessments created, and the types of activities planned.

Strategy Implementation

1. **Get to know your students.** At the beginning of the school year (or before if you can), get to know your students and their backgrounds as in-depth as possible. This includes learning about their interests, culture(s), and intersecting identities. (For more information on getting to know your students, see *Strategy 17: Connecting Skills and Content with Students' Lives and Interest* and Strategies 7 and 8 from the second book in our series, *Creating Positive Classroom Climate: 30 Practical Strategies for All School Contexts*). A few ways to get to know your students include:
   - *Student Questionnaire:* Create a questionnaire that students can fill out the first week of school. Consider including the following topics on the questionnaire:
     - Language(s) spoken
     - Religion
     - Race and ethnicity
     - Gender and preferred pronouns
     - Sexuality (for older students)
     - Socioeconomic status
     - Neuro and physical diversity
     - Country or countries of origin
     - Interests (favorite things to do)
     - Struggles
     - Desires
     - What they want to learn
     - What narratives they feel have been left out of their learning
     - Future goals

- *Family Questionnaire:* You may want to share an adapted version of the student questionnaire with students' families or caretakers. Work with your students to determine which of the categories provided should be part of the questionnaire. The questionnaire should be translated into the home language of families so they can equitably answer the questions. If families are responding in their home language and you don't speak that language, find a translator or use a translation software like Google Translate. The questionnaire should also be offered on paper or digitally to account for families that do not have access to technology or have the technological skills.
- *In-Class Activities:* During the first weeks of school, create a variety of activities that help you and the students get to know one another in different ways. Try to design activities that are a combination of silly, fun, and serious that address each of the topics on the family questionnaire. Be transparent with students that the purpose of the activities are to both help everyone learn about each other and to help you plan the course in a way that addresses the backgrounds, perspectives, and needs of each student.
- *Identity Mapping:* Have students map out all parts of their identity and how they intersect. This will help the students and you see how they exist uniquely in the world, which will enable you to adapt your curriculum to help them feel seen every day in your classroom.

UNDERSTANDING INTERSECTIONALITY

When students think about their identities, they consider many different aspects of what makes them who they are. Plan to introduce the concept of intersectionality (in an age-appropriate way) to your students so they can understand the importance and nuances of it. According to the Center for Intersectional Justice (2024), "The concept of intersectionality describes the ways in which systems of inequality based on gender, race, ethnicity, sexual orientation, gender identity, disability, class and other forms of discrimination 'intersect' to create unique dynamics and effects." Helping you and your students better understanding the intersecting parts of their identities will help you plan curricula and instruction that is more inclusive.

---

2. **Consider diverse and representative lenses for your curriculum.** Once you have a strong sense of your students, who they are, and what their assets and needs are, dive into your curriculum to see how you can help students feel seen while also introducing them to other perspectives and cultures.
   - *Not Represented:* Look at what you plan to teach and see what elements of your students are represented and what are not. For those areas where your students are not represented, see if you have a background and materials to address those topics. If you do not, take the time to learn about those areas so you can meaningfully integrate them into your class.

- For instance, if you learn that you have LGBTQIA+ students in your class and you aren't prepared to meaningfully teach them, read queer theory and LGBTQIA+ curriculum that can fills gaps in your curriculum.
- *New Lenses:* It is also important to identify what backgrounds, cultures, and perspectives are not represented within your students. Then learn about those areas—theories, histories, texts—and consider when and where to integrate them into your curriculum.
- *Where to Learn More:* You can learn about your students' cultures and backgrounds and those not represented in a variety of ways, including joining professional organizations (like National Council of Teachers of English) and attending their professional development opportunities; getting involved with Facebook, X [formerly Twitter], TikTok, and other social media teacher groups and chats; seeking out state and district professional development; creating learning communities within your school or district; talking to college professors who are experts in the lenses; and/or learning from your students and their families by asking them for resources they recommend regarding their background(s) and the parts of their identities.
- *Adapt for Age:* Once you have learned about the diverse perspectives and lenses, consider how you will adapt the material to meet the developmental needs of your students.
  - For instance, if you are teaching second graders, you can introduce racism, bias, and microaggressions, but you must select examples that seven- and eight-year-olds can relate to and understand based on their lived experiences.

With a classroom that is very diverse racially and culturally, students bring a different perspective to the class. I start talking about the different places families are from and what makes those places unique. It's not just about reading and writing, it's about understanding cultural differences related to emotions, roles, etc. Students often carry quite a bit from home and then you as the teacher can support them.

—Akiko Mazor

SHALLOW VERSUS DEEP CULTURE

When thinking about culture, people often focus on what can be seen or heard overtly rather than going deeper into what influences a person's values and actions. Often the term *cultural iceberg* (Hall, 1976) is used to describe the different levels of cultural representation: the above-water part of the iceberg represents the surface elements of culture that people easily see or hear, and the larger, below-water part of the iceberg represents the more substantial and deep elements of culture that drive behaviors and choices.

3. **Examine equitable approaches and determine all the supports students need.** After diving into the lenses and theories related to your curriculum, figure out what factors will impact delivering the content in an equitable way; you also want to evaluate how you are using an asset-based approach. When considering equity, think about:
    - *Language:* When accounting for the language diversity in your classroom, identify the different ways that your English-language learners and their families need to be supported. This may include:
        - Translated materials.
        - Using translators when communicating with families.
        - Alternative assignments or homework that enable students to achieve the same class or assignment goals while using different language skills.
    - *Neuro and Physical Diversity:* It is important to determine how to support the neuro and physical diversity in your classroom. To do this, start by following each student's Individualized Education Program (IEP) or 504 plan if they have one. Then ask yourself:
        - *Learning:* How can I modify the curriculum and offer alternative and supplementary materials to help students achieve the learning goals for the class?
        - *Physical:* How can I arrange the classroom to enable the student(s) to navigate effectively? What are the optimal seating arrangements and options? How do I integrate groups that allow for all students to collaborate most effectively?
        - *Mental and Emotional:* How do I create a safe and supportive learning environment? How do I select material that is not triggering for students? How do I create groups and organize activities where students have built-in support?
    - *Cultural Diversity:* Culture can mean many things in your classroom, including a student's race, ethnicity, and country or countries of origin. Consider the ways that culture impacts:
        - *Communication:* Different cultures have different ways of communicating and linguistic styles. Embrace each form of communication while also helping your students understand how to "code switch," where they can adapt the way they speak and communicate based on their setting to meet the expectations of that setting. Also, honor how some cultures prefer to be quiet and not make direct eye contact, whereas other cultures communicate best in loud and joking ways. Take the time to understand cultural communication norms, and consider your students' communication needs when crafting your plans.
        - *Content:* Students need to feel connected to what they are learning, so finding ways to integrate content that reflects the cultural diversity of your students

> **Avoid Tokenism**
>
> If you have only one or a few students who represent a particular background or identity, do not single them out and require that they represent everyone with their background. Rather, give them opportunities to opt-in to share when introducing and discussing the content related to their background.

is imperative. These can be texts that help students learn about the different cultures in the classroom or simply by adding anecdotes, vignettes, or word problems that integrate elements of students' cultures.
- *Socioeconomic Level:* Whether or not there is socioeconomic diversity in your classroom, it is important to help all students understand that socioeconomic diversity exists, but also support those who are in need of resources without them feeling targeted or ostracized. Consider:
  - *Resources:* If possible within your classroom or school, provide a food pantry, clothes and laundry services, school supplies, access to free before and after-school care, and free transportation.
  - *Content:* Be mindful when planning how questions may lead to students sharing examples that reflect their socioeconomic status. Consider ways to ensure that students will not feel superior or inferior based on this status. For instance, if you want students to share what they did over a school break where some of your students traveled internationally while others were unable to leave their apartment, frame the question where it is about sharing one thing that brought students joy during the break and then equally celebrate everyone's answers (you could do the same thing for sharing something sad that happened as well).
- *Gender and Sexuality:* A student's gender and sexuality is often overlooked when it comes to how students are taught and the curriculum that aligns with their needs. Some important things to address:
  - *Pronouns:* Honor students' preferred pronouns. Explicitly ask for students to identify their own pronouns, and then ensure that everyone in the class uses those pronouns when addressing them.
  - *Hidden Curriculum:* Many actions are unintentionally gendered based on how many people have been socialized. Therefore, when planning and teaching, look out for what you ask students to do (e.g., asking *all* students, and not just the males, to help carry supplies), how often you call on one gender versus the other, and how you group students.
  - *Gendering:* Be careful not to gender the learning experience in different ways. This might include having games that are boys versus girls, selecting colors that are stereotypically more for boys (blue) and girls (pink), or encouraging boys in math and science and girls in language arts.
- *Religion:* If you work in a school with religious diversity, it is important to identify which religions are practiced within your classroom to determine which holidays students celebrate, which practices and rituals students follow, and possible conflicts between religions that exist. For each:
  - *Holidays:* Recognize and celebrate each student's major holidays throughout the year and don't prioritize integrating activities for one religion over another. For instance, there are multiple winter holidays, but if Christmas is the only holiday honored and celebrated, it becomes challenging for all students who do not celebrate.

- *Practices and Rituals:* Be aware of all important practices and rituals that impact your students' daily experience, including things such as dietary restrictions, prayer needs, or clothing students wear.
- *Conflict:* We live in a world where there is often conflict between religions. This can become a challenge when students enter the classroom, so be intentional in planning your class and creating a space where students can celebrate their differences rather than fight over those differences.

> **Stay Neutral to Be Inclusive**
>
> Be neutral with different projects and perspectives; it's important to be inclusive of many different perspectives.
>
> —*Akiko Mazor*

4. **Select inclusive texts ("windows," "mirrors," and "sliding glass doors").** Once you have a clear sense of who your students are, how to adapt your curriculum, and how you need to plan for equity and multiple perspectives, it is time to select inclusive texts for your classroom. The goal is to have an inclusive set of voices and perspectives that provide (Bishop, 1990): "windows" for students to get a sense of the lives and experiences of others, "mirrors" where students see texts that reflect themselves, and "sliding glass doors" that students/readers can walk through to make connections with these other and diverse worlds and perspectives. To do this:
   - *Core and Supplemental Texts:* You want to ensure that all three types of texts are included as core/mentor texts (if you have the power to make those decisions) and supplemental texts and account for students' explicit and hidden identities (like mental health and neurodiversity). Help students recognize the importance of seeing new perspectives while giving them mirrors of their own. Try to find texts where the author is writing from the experience themselves (own-voice texts) and include characters that reflect a range of experiences as well. Select texts that celebrate individuals as people and not just their trauma.
   - *Access to Texts:* If you don't have the access or funds to get inclusive texts you can critically analyze noninclusive texts to evaluate why and how they are not inclusive and what can be done to change them to be more inclusive. For instance, point out when students are not represented in texts or accurately represented.

5. **Develop instructional strategies around the teaching of varied lenses.** Be intentional about the instructional strategies you use to infuse equitable and diverse perspectives.
   - *Integrate Opportunities for Analysis, Discussion, and Comparison:* One of the best ways to infuse multiple perspectives in an equitable way is to make the learning student-centered where students are challenged to analyze each perspective, compare them, and engage in meaningful and productive dialogue. Be

sure to frame the introduction of different perspectives through an asset-based lens where students learn to celebrate differences and challenge diverse perspectives in ways that help all students understand where others are coming from. Turn-and-talks and small-group discussion are a great way to get students discussing different perspectives.
- *Mini-Lessons and Jigsaws:* Take time to use mini-lessons to introduce new perspectives, but do it in a way that is student-driven. Then once students have a context, consider using jigsaw activities where students become experts in one perspective and then teach one another about other perspectives.

6. **Develop inclusive assessment(s) addressing multiple perspectives.** Beyond making instruction inclusive, it is important to design assessments that reflect the multiple perspectives students learned and ensure they are accessible to all students. To do that:
   - *Offer Options:* When possible, include options where students can address what they have learned from one of multiple lenses.
   - *Account for Accommodations:* Either design your assessment with the accommodations your students require, or offer alternative assessments with the accommodations that still help students demonstrate mastery of the assessment's goal(s).
   - *Be Creative:* Think outside the box, and consider designing assessments that are tied to the world outside of school and that can be done using diverse media.
   - *Make It Inquiry-Based:* Design assessments where students are solving problems to demonstrate their knowledge of the content and not just providing facts.

7. **Maintain communication.** To ensure you continue to offer multiple perspectives and fill in gaps in your students' learning, it is important to maintain communication with both your students and their families. Some ways to do that include:
   - *Students:* At minimum, every couple of months, use follow-up questionnaires with your students to have them let you know what they feel is missing from the curriculum and how they can be better supported.
   - *Families:* There are a number of ways to engage in meaningful communication with families. Consider:
     - Provide opportunities for families to come to class to celebrate the work the students have been doing. During these events, pay attention to how your students interact with their families and others to account for cultural differences in communication.
     - During parent-teacher conferences, and other communication with families throughout the year, ask their thoughts on what is missing from the curriculum.

When discussing topics that are counter beliefs at home, ground the discussion in the human rights of all individuals and the humanity of all individuals. You can use www.learningforjustice.org standards that can be adapted that are very skill-based.

—*Rachel Scupp-Jorge*

- For families new to the school, prioritize reaching out to families who are having a hard time adjusting to the school.
- Maintain consistent communication in any way you can including online classroom management platforms like "ClassDojo," phone calls home, and meetings in person.

Bringing Families and Their Diverse Cultures into the Classroom

I have parents come into the classroom to share parts of their culture. This begins discussions about race, diversity, and how history has informed it. I want every student to feel represented in the classroom and ensure there is a representative to come for a family gathering to share elements of their culture. Then I start talking about holidays, beyond Christmas and Chanukah, and include discussion about Eid and Lunar New Year and other cultures and religions. This leads to more students opening up about sharing all of their holidays and not just the "Hallmark holidays." This shifts what you focus on to be more inclusive and encourages students to share details and experiences of the different holidays. All students can then celebrate with one another and the students and teacher are learning together.

—Akiko Mazor

STRATEGY IN ACTION: PUTTING AN INCLUSIVE CURRICULUM INTO ACTION

The process of developing theoretical close reading lenses began in 2017 as a collaboration between Dr. Emily Meixner from The College of New Jersey and my school district. We pitched a pilot curriculum to teach LGBTQ Middle Grade novels using Queer Theory, and our work was quickly adopted district-wide by the eighth-grade teachers. As a result of this unit, I transformed my instruction to lead with theoretical close reading lenses across all other genres of analysis, specifically in connection to our social justice book club and genocide units.

In its first iteration, the LGBTQ unit led to the establishment of a Gay Straight Alliance at the middle school level; promoted agency, advocacy, and acceptance among students; and led to more opportunities for empowerment in inclusivity. Since the adoption of the unit district-wide, students have hosted the first ever Gay, Lesbian, and Straight Education Network conference at a middle school in New Jersey, removed gender-specific placards from single-stall restrooms to reflect gender neutrality, hosted an equity and inclusion conference at the high school, and advocated for a multitude of issues by taking actionable steps to promote change.

Students have received responses from politicians, leaders, presidents, CEOs, organizations, and other leading members of our local, national, and global communities. Students have also developed skills to become empowered through agency and to take action for the issues they hope to improve. As a result of this work, students at the high school have developed a social justice course, multiple social justice and equity clubs, and have worked closely with administration to promote equity and inclusion across the district.

—Rachel Scupp-Jorge

> **WHY I LIKE THIS STRATEGY**
>
> It is imperative for me to know about students and their families in every aspect (social, economic, educational, support system, family dynamics to name a few!). This information really guides me to modify my approach to not only my teaching, but also my interactions with students and their families. I'm not just a teacher, I'm learning at the same time.
>
> —*Akiko Mazor*
>
> Using theoretical lenses to teach with equity and multiple perspectives (1) allows students to process information in an academic context while also positioning themselves in social justice activism, (2) increases rigor through the analysis of text, (3) elevates domain-specific vocabulary and content knowledge, (4) protects teachers in analyzing inclusive literature, texts, and content by incorporating analytical framework alongside advocacy, and (5) fulfills Core Curricular Content Standards while also introducing Social Justice Standards to the English Curriculum. It's hard to do this shift to using a theoretical lens and using the skills as the backbone of your teaching initially. Then once you do it, you don't want to do it any other way. It will take work, but you recognize how important it is, and it's life affirming work for students who have never seen themselves represented in literature.
>
> —*Rachel Scupp-Jorge*

Adaptation for Different Assets and Needs

Cultural Diversity	
Limited Diversity	*Lots of Diversity*
*Focus on building in windows and sliding glass doors into your curriculum through texts, videos, and activities.	*Ensure texts, videos, and other materials consistently mirror the students in your class while also having students collaborate to see through the windows of their peers.
*Find ways to integrate elements of different cultures into each unit by focusing on highlighting different positive cultural events relevant to the content or time of year.	*Integrate more jigsaw-style activities where students can learn from one another.

Curricular Freedom	
Limited Freedom	*Lots of Freedom*
*Add as many supplemental texts and materials as you can to provide more perspectives.	*Ensure that most lessons use texts and materials that include windows, mirrors, and sliding glass doors.
*Find ways to integrate elements of different cultures into the activities and assessments that enhance the required curriculum.	*Create assessments that relate to the lived experiences of the students and challenge them to understand multiple perspectives.

STRATEGY IN ACTION: HERITAGE DOLLS PROJECT AS SPRINGBOARD TO AN INCLUSIVE CLASSROOM

After having our first parent-teacher conference, I usually have a good picture of each student and their family. I then give students a family project called "Heritage Dolls." I ask families to dress up a paper cutout doll with some materials that reflect their cultural background.

When I introduce the project, we discuss the differences we notice in our clothing, the food we eat, and the places our families come from.

After students complete their Heritage Dolls, each of them shows and tells about which country their families are from. Then I invite the families in to see the dolls by having a class Thanksgiving/Multicultural Feast. For the feast, I asked families to bring some traditional food from their home county. Over the years, I modified this part to accommodate busy families and economically disadvantaged families by giving them the choice to send in some utensils or paper plates instead of food. This ensures that families do not feel pressured to cook something or spend much to participate. I have also made special arrangements with some families to help them participate.

I have had many successful years in the past. A successful year meant that I had every family participate in some way. Families are able to see gorgeous heritage dolls on the bulletin board and appreciate the wide range of culture we can share together as a classroom community. I have seen families often complimenting each other. Students are also proud to show their hard work to their families in the classroom.

Through this project, my hope is that students will learn about their own family background and their peers' background as well, which will lead to the students accepting differences.

I then build on the Heritage Dolls project and feast in December when the holiday season comes by focusing on celebrations with families rather than specific holidays. I introduce Christmas, Hanukkah, Eid, Lunar New Year, birthdays, and any special holidays depending on different cultural backgrounds. I emphasize that we all celebrate special days with families.

Then I continue by teaching students what families are. We learn about different types of families, and I make sure to address many different family situations to students I have. We discuss that families are people we care for and love. Then I conclude that we also can be a classroom family, even though we are not related, but we care for each other.

Finally, in the spring, we walk the neighborhood, so students can see many of the differences we have been studying and discussing in class. This includes: different restaurants, languages/alphabets, focus on ethnic enclaves, family units, and religious beliefs. This helps us go deeper into each of these areas so students can better understand and appreciate the diversities in our community.

—*Akiko Mazor*

STRATEGY 20: USING LEARNING MANAGEMENT SYSTEMS TO ORGANIZE YOUR LESSONS

> **Teacher Contributors**
> *Jeff Bradbury, Teachercast (CT), Kindergarten–12th grades*
> *Kristin Donley, Arapahoe Ridge High School (CO), 9th–12th grades*

Learning management systems (LMS) are software applications or web-based technologies that enable educators to organize, plan, and execute instruction remotely and in-person. LMS are accessible to both students and parents/guardians. Learning how to effectively use LMS as a planning tool will make the planning process more seamless, keep you organized, allow for easier adaptations from year to year, save time, increase student feedback and accessibility, and help enhance creativity and technology integration into your plans. It also keeps all of the learning in one place for educators, students, and parents/guardians. The following are examples of commonly used LMS: Blackboard, Canvas, Edmodo, Google Classroom, Moodle, Schoology, and Seesaw.

Strategy Implementation

1. **Talk to experienced LMS users.** Using an LMS can be a daunting task if you are new to it. Therefore, speak with an experienced LMS user who can walk you through the basics of how the LMS works, how they use it, how it benefits their students, and struggles they have with it. Ask them any and all questions you have; bounce ideas off them; get new ideas; have them critique and provide advice on your ideas, etc. You can find LMS experts in multiple ways:
   - *Your School/District:* Find multiple people in your district who have experience working with the LMS you are trying to use. By talking to more than one person, you are likely to learn different ways in which people use the LMS as well as a variety of tricks to adapt it to your needs.
   - *Online Communities:* There are numerous online communities you can join to learn more about many LMS. These include YouTube, TikTok, and LMS Help Centers.
   - *Education Technology Conferences:* Attend local and state educational technology conferences where there will be experts on most LMS used in schools.

2. **Explore LMS Uses.** Once you have a basic understanding of the LMS you plan to use from your discussion(s) with experienced users, take time getting to know the settings within the platform, and play with all the functionality options. Make sure to:
   - Look at samples provided.
   - Explore each section within the LMS.
   - Test out of the tool options.
   - Write down anything that you definitely want to use when you set up your course.
   - Write down anything that confuses you or you need someone to help you answer.

3. **Decide what works for you.** After getting a sense of the LMS, take time to figure out why and how you want to use the LMS to best support you, your students, and their families. You want this tool to work for you rather than you working to try to formulate your approach to fit the tool.

4. **Work backward.** Develop concrete goals for your LMS use, and then start to build out your LMS keeping each of those goals in mind. But don't be afraid to change the goals or elements of your LMS as you realize new and better ways to maximize its use for everyone's benefit. Goals might include easier accessibility to class materials, streamlined communication with students and their families, or more showcasing of students' work.

5. **Figure out naming conventions.** A large part of LMS is making the learning and materials accessible. Along with that comes the need for users to search for materials; therefore, how you name files and sections on the platform is important. To maximize searchability in your LMS, ensure that you are consistent with how you name files and sections so a user can use one search term to find what they need (e.g., if you have a class section "103" make sure you name each file "103" and not "Class 103"). If you name similar files different ways, it can make it difficult for users to locate what they need.

6. **Use your syllabus to organize course materials.** This is the most time-consuming and important step with your LMS set up because it makes your LMS accessible to all of its users. Use your syllabus as a roadmap for putting together your LMS. When organizing, consider:
   - *Calendar:* If your whole school uses the same LMS and you have access to your colleagues' calendars through the LMS, use this information to ensure you are aware of when your students have other large assignments due. Use your class calendar to post all important assignments and due dates, which should link to the assignment and its accompanying materials.
     - NOTE: Using these calendars will help students develop time management skills. The embedded calendars in the LMS help students see what is coming (short and long term), and it also allows for text and email reminders to students about assignments. This helps students understand a schedule (for kindergarten–3rd grade this is less structured, and for 4th–12th grades, it can be to help students self-manage more effectively).
   - *Course Themes and Subthemes:* Determine each theme or topic you are using in your course and each subtheme or topic. Then create folders, and add the corresponding materials for each of those folders. This could be done based on each class you teach, units, assessments, lessons, assignments, and so on.
   - *Scaffolding Resources:* Think about how to break down the course material in ways that help all of your students connect with what they are learning. Consider:
     - Different supports each of your students need and the best modalities to help them succeed. These may include graphic organizers, readings to build background knowledge, links to videos on related skills, and so on.

- The number of options or additional resources you need to provide for each experience to aid students in meeting your goals for that experience.
  - NOTE: To create these options or additional resources, you can create a baseline lesson, activities, and materials, and then copy and paste them to make tweaks and different versions that students can access to meet their learning needs. A great thing about this embedded differentiation is that students cannot tell what other students are accessing and using, which creates a safer, more equitable learning environment for everyone in your classroom.
- The best media to convey material that helps students access and understand what they are learning from different perspectives.
- Diverse assignments students can complete related to the same prompt/task where students have more than one choice in how to complete the assignment.

LMS and Equity

I got into using LMS because of equity; students with very different needs can benefit from accessing curriculum 24/7. Work is never lost; you need a place that is a record of information. You have a record that can be improved upon and added to and you don't lose it over time. Every teacher has a good starting point and every kid can access it whenever they want (notes, resources, etc.), and it lets families know what you're teaching and where to find it. Plus, video and audio and transcript really help with hearing impaired and ADHD students because it's closed captioned and they can pause it on their own.

—*Kristin Donley*

- *General Resources/Resource Center:* Design a place where you can add materials to help make the LMS more accessible for all of the users. This includes tutorial videos on using different elements of the LMS and additional resources on the content and skill development of your course from vetted places and sources. Each subfolder in your resource center should be clearly labeled for easy access.
- *Standards-Based Grading:* LMS are often a great tool to use standards-based grading. Check the LMS you are using to see if you are able to create assessments that link directly to your standards. If this is possible, some LMSs (like Schoology) allow you to click on a button that will color-code how students did on each question of the assessment based on the linked standard (provide a green if they met the standard, a yellow if they are approaching the standard, and a red if they are still developing in that standard). This makes the learning and assessments more visible and accessible for students so they can see, in a positive way, how they are progressing toward the standards.

- *Existing Websites and Resources:* LMS allow you to integrate resources like teacher websites and other course-management systems that you already have.
  - For example, you can use Google Classroom within Schoology as a "one-stop shop" where all the links you need can be found in one site.

Standards-Based Grading and LMS

Using standards-based grading through Schoology (my LMS) really helped students see what they can do, which is positive. They knew what they were learning and what they needed to develop, and they became their own advocates. Students were in learning pits where they couldn't catch up, but with standards-based learning, they see they have some mastery and just need to build. They can say, "I need help with this part of the standard," and as they work toward mastering it, they see they are getting it because they see it turning green; and they're used to games like that. You can also assign badges once they gain that mastery; you can say, "you did it and got this badge!," and they get really excited. I would also sometimes give them tangible incentives from the dollar store (like bubbles) that they get when they get their mastery badges too, and that really got students motivated. You can do this easily through most LMS.

—*Kristin Donley*

USING LMS FOR DATA GATHERING, INTERACTIVE ASSESSMENT ANALYSIS, AND FEEDBACK

When you use your LMS for students to complete assessments, most LMS will then store all the student data. With this information, the LMS can:

- Tell you how many students answered specific questions.
- Evaluate rubrics and how people did and store historical data on the assessment from year to year.
- Do cross-correlations to evaluate how students are doing and how to better support students over time. It will pull up graphs for you and compare students across years and classes.

You can tweak future lessons based on previous students' performance because better data drives better instructional choices.

The LMS can also help provide stronger feedback. For instance, using their device's microphone, students can talk to the teacher to ask questions (which really helps shy students and students who don't have extra time). Students can send messages 24/7 by text or recording their voice and sending it through the LMS. This enables you to give feedback in real time.

But don't forget to set limits for when you are available to your students so you have work-life balance and get some sleep! This is also important because it serves as a model for your students.

—*Kristin Donley*

- *Discussion Boards:* Using strategic discussion boards can be a great way to make your LMS interactive and provide support for your students. You can do this by setting up discussions like "Tutoring Center" where students can have a safe place to ask one another questions and for help with work they are doing in class. (You can also enter these discussions from time to time to answer questions students may have difficulty answering for one another.)
  - NOTE: Before having students engage in discussion board posts, explicitly teach students etiquette for how to communicate with one another safely and kindly.

7. **Be creative.** Use the technological capabilities of the LMS to design and create experiences for your students that elevate how they interact with what they are learning. For instance, have students do a Jigsaw activity where they can learn about a topic in-depth, and then post what they learn in some creative way like photo essays, video clips, or Google Slides. Next, create a scavenger hunt so students can explore and learn about what other students studied by setting up a feature where students can see each other's work.

8. **Test each element of the LMS.** After you have built out your LMS, go through each part of it to test that it works as you intended. Then after it works to your liking, have colleagues who have worked with the LMS before try to navigate your course to give feedback on what works well for them and what they believe needs to be improved and tweaked. Lastly, if you have a student or students who you know and trust from previous years, consider having them navigate your LMS course to give feedback as well.

Increase Collaboration!

Many districts provide a scope and sequence for you to follow. Then through an LMS, you can create a lesson where multiple teachers can collaborate on a lesson (like on a Google Doc), and everyone with access to your district's LMS has the access to resources and can pull it into their classrooms. Some districts even have their teachers write the district's scope and sequence together through the LMS. In all, LMS allows for great collaboration on curriculum!

---

9. **Teach students and families how to use the LMS.** It is important to start every year by providing students and their families with a tutorial to help them understand your LMS course, how you expect students to use and navigate it, and to practice using it. This can be done in class with your students during the first week of classes and through an Open House organized by the school or you directly with the parents.

> **Using LMS to Communicate with Students and Families**
>
> At my school's Open House, I show families how to log into Schoology, find the classes, etc. and to learn what their child is actually learning and doing. Families see that they have access to the work their child submits. LMS can provide a ping when a student submits something and then family members, teachers, and administrators can comment on it.
>
> It's all about positive feedback—parents are so appreciative of this changed narrative. It's so important to be transparent with families about what you are actually doing. For example, there's an email function where you can share work you're really proud of with students and their families; it's changing the conversation to be more of a positive behavioral support.
>
> Parents and guardians have said that it creates more conversations at the dining room table. They can have deeper conversations about learning at home. Parents/guardians are part of that learning community and LMS help facilitate these conversations with students and families. This open communication with families also enables them to provide suggestions about how to be more equitable; they offer more help and connections like volunteering to come in!
>
> —*Kristin Donley*

10. **Build the LMS from year to year.** Any class you teach is permanently archived. It is lots of work in your first year to build a LMS course and all its materials, but after that first year, it is archived, and you can just tweak and adapt it from year to year moving forward.

STRATEGY IN ACTION: BUILDING YOUR OWN LMS

A few years ago, I put together a teacher website where everything is designed and built in one place with all of my projects. Because I never want to be the guy that says, "You want to see something, hold on. Go to Google Drive, and then go to this." Instead, I put all of my course material on one website and platform where, if I pull up a particular project on the site, everything is there that I'm doing for the lesson; students can walk themselves through what they need to do.

I also build my personal LMS for the families. With my LMS, I can email the family and say, "We're doing student biographies, click 'here' to help your child." You can let them know that all of the slides they need are in this one place, as well as any additional resources, outlines, videos, and other resources, including possible translations into other languages students and their families might speak.

I add the materials into Google Drive folders embedded into the website, where I label and name each file so students and families can search for the title of the assignment and then all of the accompanying documents will pop down so they can easily find and access them. For instance, I created a "Who Am I" assignment where I labeled each part of the assignment and resources for the assignment beginning with "Who Am I," which helped me stay organized and my students and their families have easy access to the files.

This has saved me time because, if I want to teach this, now it's all in one Google Drive folder. So, you're creating yourself a system now—that yes, it takes a long time to initially create—but it saves you time in the future. I would rather be with my family in August at the Disney Park instead of recreating assignments and planning things anew for the upcoming school year. You don't have to start each school year trying to figure out what was that lesson I taught last year that I spent a lot of time creating. Instead, having your own LMS, it's all on this site and I have every single thing that I did, and on top of that, here's my name, here's my room, here's my welcome message, here's my contact, and here's the calendar. It's like walking through a social media story on your phone, which is how parents and guardians would see it.

All I'm trying to do with the LMS is inspire users to learn. So I ask myself, "how can I create a system where I can be more hands on with students and less preachy at the beginning of the day?" And my teacher website is the answer, because everything students are doing in class is built into the site. All I have to do is walk in and say, "All right everyone, here we go." Then I'll talk for a couple seconds and the slides are there for students to get started with their "Do Now" (and subsequent assignments); it puts the ownership of the work on the students. I've been showing my LMS to teachers and students for the last couple of years, and every time I do, people are saying, "that's pretty cool!"

—Jeff Bradbury

WHY I LIKE THIS STRATEGY

Using a LMS puts everything on a platform where you are creating online teaching materials, not just for students, but also for families at home to see and be able to support their children when needed. It also teaches the parents how to use the resources and lets them know what is available to support their children.

—*Jeff Bradbury*

If leveraged appropriately, a quality LMS can take much of the load off of a teacher so they can focus on differentiation, student feedback, and building relationships. A quality LMS can help a teacher easily track standards mastery, build scaffolded and differentiated lessons, provide better ways for 2-way family communication and student feedback, and link in resources to fill gaps (intervention and extension).

—*Kristin Donley*

Adaptation for Different Assets and Needs

Comfort with Technology

Limited Comfort
- Start simple by making folders with links and other resources, helping you to go paperless. Then each year, add one or two things to improve on as a teacher like feedback and communication integration.
- Focus professional development on learning about LMS through Teaching Channel, YouTube, and other resources.

Lots of Comfort
- Focus on your next goal, and look at tools and the professional development you need to learn it.
- Become an LMS leader at your school where you support colleagues with less comfort using LMS.

Access to School-Wide LMS

No Access
- Look for free LMS options.
- When you need that "Pro" option, contact the company for an extended trial, and then go to your district to convince them to adopt. Offer to do a trial and then promote it.
- You can turn a teacher website into an LMS, but it requires more technology knowledge. (See *Strategy in Action: Building Your Own LMS*.)

Access
- Create a teacher collaborative group focused on LMS use. In your group, share best practices, resources, and support one another in learning new tools and uses for best LMS practices.
- Reach out to other schools or districts that use the same LMS to see how they optimize its use across the school.

> **STRATEGY IN ACTION: USING A LMS TO PROVIDE QUALITY FEEDBACK ON THE GO**
>
> There are so many ways one can leverage an LMS. I am a science teacher and have used LMS for my classes, for clubs I sponsor, and for faculty professional development. This has helped me save time and provide quality feedback to students.
>
> My LMS has the capability of recording feedback. As a parent, I am taking my own children to music and sports practices, which limits how much time I have to grade and give feedback, unless I want to drag around a huge stack of unwieldy papers. Once I started using a quality LMS, I found that I could grade on the go. My LMS has an app with a microphone feature. I simply look at student science lab reports in the LMS and am able to give voice feedback on sections for student improvement.
>
> My students love this method. First with hard copies, they often lost them or left them in the classroom to never be seen again. Second, voice feedback remains in the system, so when students are ready to work on rewrites, they can listen to my comments, ask more questions if needed through the system, and easily turn in rewrites any time of the day. This method has opened up more time for in-class discussions and specific questions from students. Finally, I've noticed students actually look forward to my voice feedback and are disappointed if they don't get as much on an assignment. In other words, on hard copies, they barely paid attention to the feedback, but in the LMS, they seemed to focus and notice it more, and actually looked forward to it!
>
> —*Kristin Donley*

Sample Materials

Online Discussion Guidelines

You are engaging in an online discussion with your peers. Below are some tips to make this experience meaningful and collaborative.

1. **Be Unique:** Share ideas that are unique to you.
2. **Cite:** If you make a connection to an outside source, be sure to share a link or citation.
3. **Critique Ideas:** Offer feedback and critiques that are about people's ideas and not about them as individuals.
4. **Be Respectful:** Choose your words and your tone carefully. (This includes the font, CAPS, and emojis you decide to use.)
5. **Reserve Judgement:** Ask questions to clarify what you may want to judge. Sometimes gathering more information helps you expand your perspective.
6. **Pause before Posting:** Whatever you post will be read by a larger audience, so represent yourself well. Think, reread, edit before you post.

Chapter Five

10 Bonus Strategies

In these final pages, you will find 10 bonus strategies that require small steps for implementation but make a huge impact. Sometimes, teacher candidates and newer teachers benefit from having these teacher moves made explicit. For more seasoned teachers, some of these strategies may seem like teacher moves that are second nature, and if that is the case, hopefully seeing them on this list serves as an affirmation of good practice!

1. **Keep it Simple**
   When planning, don't overcomplicate things. If you are coming up with an activity or concept that feels overly complex, break it down into its basic components so it is as clear as possible. Remember, if something is confusing to you, it will definitely be confusing for your students. Also, to keep your planning process simple, if you are struggling with what to do with your plans and feel stuck, move on to a part of the plan that comes easier to you. Then once you have fleshed out the easier parts of the plan, return to where you were stuck, and you will likely be able to come up with something that fits well with the rest of the plan you just created.

2. **Keeping Track of Strategies and Activities**
   As you plan out your units and lessons, keep track of the types of strategies and activities you use with your students. This can be done by creating a unit calendar that outlines each day's activities and strategies. When looking over your unit calendar, ensure that you use a variety of strategies with your students each week, return to strategies that work well, and find opportunities to refine and give newer strategies a second or third try.

3. **Schedule Learning around School Breaks**
   Continuity is an important factor in teaching and learning. Therefore, whenever possible, develop a logical stopping point in any unit you are teaching before a school break. If you have a long unit that cannot end before a break, consider dividing the larger unit into smaller mini-units. To do this, end one of the mini-units before the break, and when you return from break, start the next mini-unit that

builds on the previous one. When introducing the next mini-unit or starting a new unit, reinforce what students have previously learned, and build on that knowledge so students can move forward effectively and efficiently.

4. **Borrow and Adapt**
   Great teaching is often borrowing and adapting ideas. When planning new units and lessons, see what else has been done on those topics before through colleagues, social media (Facebook, TikTok, X [formerly Twitter], Instagram), content and pedagogy books, blogs, and through professional development opportunities. Then determine which ideas, strategies, and activities would be a great fit for your classroom, and figure out how they need to be adapted to align with your students' specific needs. Lastly, don't forget to give credit to the original source of your idea when you use it in your classroom.

5. **Look Back and Plan Forward**
   After teaching a lesson and unit, take note of what works and changes you want to make in the future. This can be in the form of a journal, or you can take notes directly on your unit and lesson plans based on what you just taught while also making revisions on future plans based on your critical reflections. These notes can be about immediate and short-term revisions to plans or about plans you hope to make in the long-term future when you teach the material again.

6. **Stay Organized**
   Planning can be overwhelming, especially when teaching multiple subjects or preps and from year to year. Therefore, figure out a system that works for you to keep your planning and its components organized. It can be helpful to break down your plans into unit folders that have subfolders for lesson plans, assessments, and materials. To ensure you don't lose your work, use a cloud-based platform (like Google Drive, iCloud, etc.), and not just on a flash drive, where you keep your work saved at all times. It can also be helpful for some to have hard copies saved in binders; but remember, binders can be ruined or lost.

7. **Team Planning**
   Planning can be greatly enhanced when done collaboratively. If your school does not build team planning into your schedule, find ways to meet and collaborate with teachers who teach the same content, teach the same grade and students, and colleagues in different disciplines that can help you create an interdisciplinary curriculum that will greatly benefit your students. Team planning can be done informally or formally (ideally both). Schedule time to collaborate with your colleagues, at least once a month if possible. Discuss your current and future plans, get meaningful feedback, and intentionally create interdisciplinary plans where students can see and understand continuity across subject areas.

8. **Weekly Planning**
   It's helpful to have your plans ready before each week and not be reliant on planning day to day (night to night). However, as you know, plans change based on what happens in class each day. Therefore, go into each week with your first three lessons planned out more completely, but keep your final two lessons of the week more as outlines where you can fill in the details—and adapt the plans—based on what happens during the first few days of the week.

9. **Planning for Adaptation** (Be OK with scrapping and changing plans.)
   Go into your planning knowing that plans often need to change. This doesn't mean that you don't plan thorough and meaningful units and lessons; rather, it means that you need to be open and OK with scrapping and adapting your plans when you realize these changes need to happen for the sake of your students. Remember, if you need to remove an activity or idea you love because it just doesn't make sense at the time, create a "parking lot" of activities and ideas you want to use in the future that you can return to when you are looking for great future ideas.

10. **Time Management and Efficient Planning**
    Everyone works differently. It is important to learn how you work most effectively and efficiently to save time and energy with your planning. To do this, play around with strategies for planning until you find what works best for you. This might include starting with outlining, setting timers for quick writes where you write down ideas until the timer goes off, using unit calendars before planning lessons, or only planning during your most productive times of the day.

Conclusion

This book was developed as a resource that would be useful for *all* teachers in *all* settings. Hopefully the details in the step-by-step description of the strategies help you to make your planning meaningful and efficient.

NOW WHAT?

Remember to take a culturally responsive/sustaining approach to using these strategies. To do this, ask yourself:

- What do I know about my students?
- How can I plan to best meet my students' learning needs?

Further, be sure to integrate these strategies with clear intention and explicit explanation of *why* you are doing what you are doing. Keeping your *why* in mind will help you think critically about your planning and the types of learning you want to support. After trying a new planning strategy, take time to reflect. Consider:

- What worked well? Why?
- What changes might you make?
- How could you adapt the strategy to better fit your needs?

Most strategies will need to be adapted in some way to fit your classroom. Hopefully the adaptations listed in each strategy are helpful in guiding your thinking. You might consider applying an adaptation from one chapter to a strategy in another chapter. If you are struggling with how to change a strategy, reach out to a colleague, or connect with fellow educators at:

Website: https://buildyourteachingtoolbox.com/
X (formerly Twitter): @BuildTeachTool
Instagram: @buildteachingtoolbox
Facebook: Build Your Teaching Toolbox

AND THEN?

Practice! Practice! Practice! How do you get better at anything? You practice! Practice new strategies until you feel confident using them when you plan. Practice adapting strategies. Practice reaching out to colleagues for support, advice, or to be cheered on for your efforts.

Perhaps you are reading this book and thinking, "Hey! I've got some great strategies that can be adapted for varied classroom settings! How do I get my ideas in a book?" Glad you asked! Please, join the toolbox sharing community at:

Website: https://buildyourteachingtoolbox.com/
Email: info@buildteachtool.com
Twitter: @BuildTeachTool
Instagram: @buildteachingtoolbox
Facebook: Build Your Teaching Toolbox

Remember, this is the third book in the five-book *Building Your Teaching Toolbox* series! Check out *Adaptable Teaching: 30 Practical Strategies for All School Contexts* (2022) and *Creating Positive Classroom Climate: 30 Practical Strategies for All School Contexts* (2022), and be on the lookout for our upcoming books on instruction and professional development.

All books in this series include step-by-step instructions for implementing/applying strategies, narratives of the *Strategy in Action*, teacher explanations of why they like each strategy, examples of how to modify the strategy based on related assets and needs, and modifications based on grade level (elementary, middle, high) and different populations of students (those who are in special education or Gifted and Talented or are English-language learners).

In addition to creating a book that could be a strong resource for teachers in varied settings and at different points in their career, all of our books are written with the hope that they will draw you in as readers and help you feel like a part of a larger community of educators who are eager to share and grow together. Please keep the community growing by providing feedback and new ideas at the email address, website, or social media platforms for the *Building Your Teaching Toolbox* community listed previously. Thank you for joining the toolbox community!

References

About universal design for learning. CAST. (2024, March 28). https://www.cast.org/impact/universal-design-for-learning-udl

ASCD. (2019, March 16). Students have to Maslow before they can Bloom. *Twitter*. https://twitter.com/ascd/status/1106937108940406789?lang=en

Bear, G. G. (2015). Preventive and classroom-based strategies. In E. T. Emmer and E. J. Sabornie (Eds.), *Handbook of classroom management* (2nd ed., pp. 15–39). New York, NY: Routledge.

Bloom, B. S. (1956). *Taxonomy of educational objectives, handbook I: The cognitive domain*. Philadelphia, PA: David McKay Co Inc.

Boykin, A. W., and Noguera, P. (2011). *Creating the opportunity to learn: Moving from research to practice to close the achievement gap*. Alexandria, VA: Association for Supervision and Curriculum Development.

Burke, J. (2023). *Teaching better day by day: A planner to support your instruction, well-being, and professional learning*. Oakland, CA: Corwin.

Cartledge, G., Lo, Y., Vincent, C. G., and Robinson-Ervin, P. (2015). Culturally responsive classroom management. In E. T. Emmer and E. J. Sabornie (Eds.), *Handbook of classroom management* (2nd ed., pp. 411–430). New York, NY: Routledge.

Cavallo, A. M., and Marek, E. (1997). T*he learning cycle: Elementary school science and beyond* . Portsmouth, NH: Heinemann.

Center for Intersectional Justice. (2024). What is intersectionality? https://www.intersectionaljustice.org/what-is-intersectionality#:~:text=The%20concept%20of%20intersectionality%20describes,create%20unique%20dynamics%20and%20effects.

Connolly, M., and Davis, J. R. (2022). *Creating positive classroom climate: 30 practical strategies for all school contexts*. Lanham, MD: Rowman & Littlefield.

Darling Hammond, L. (2015) Want to close the achievement gap? Close the teaching gap. *American Educator*, 38, 4, 14–18

Davis, J. R. (2017). *Classroom management in teacher education programs*. Cham, Switzerland: Palgrave Macmillan.

Davis, J. R., and Connolly, M. (2022). *Adaptable Teaching: 30 practical strategies for all school contexts*. Lanham, MD: Rowman & Littlefield.

Doran, G. T. (1981). There's a SMART way to write management's goals and objectives. *Journal of Management Review*, 70, 35–36.

Duncan-Andrade, J. (2011). *Growing roses in concrete*. TEDxGoldenGateED, September 28, 2011. https://www.youtube.com/watch?v=2CwS60ykM8s

Elias, M. J., Zins, J. E., Weissberg, R. P., et al. (1997). *Promoting social and emotional learning.* https://earlylearningfocus.org/wp-content/uploads/2019/12/promoting-social-and-emotional-learning-1.pdf

Gay, G. (2010). *Culturally responsive teaching: Theory, research, and practice.* New York, NY: Teachers College Press.

Ginott, H. (1972) *Teacher and child.* New York, NY: Macmillan.

Gutiérrez, K. D., and Rogoff, B. (2003). Cultural ways of learning: Individual traits or repertoires of practice. *Educational Researcher, 32*(5), 19–25. doi:10.3102/0013189x032005019

Gutstein, E., Lipman, P., Hernández, P., and de los Reyes, R. (1997). Culturally relevant mathematics teaching in a Mexican American context. *Journal for Research in Mathematics Education, 28,* 709–37. doi:10.2307/749639

Hall, E. T. (1976). *Beyond culture.* Garden City, NY: Doubleday.

Keller, J. M. (2010). *Motivational design for learning and performance: The ARCS model approach.* New York, NY: Springer.

Ladson-Billings, G. (1995). Towards a culturally relevant theory of pedagogy. *American Educational Research Journal, 32,* 465–91.

Lasic, T. (n.d.). *Maslow before bloom.* Human Edublogs. Retrieved July 10, 2020, from https://human.edublogs.org/2009/08/11/maslow-before-bloom/

Lowrey, K. A., and Classen, A. (2019) Exploring ways to support preservice teachers' use of UDL in planning and instruction. *Journal of Educational Research and Practice, 9,* 1, 261–81.

Maslow, A. H. (1943). A theory of human motivation. *Psychological Review, 4*(50): 370–96.

McLaughlin, J. H., and Bryan, L. A. (2003). Learning from rural Mexican schools about commitment and work. *Theory Into Practice, 42*(4), 289–95.

Miklova, S. (2021). Strategies for effective lesson planning. *Center for Research on Teaching and Learning.* https://crlt.umich.edu/gsis/p2_5

Miller, J. (n.d.). Gotta "Maslow" before you "bloom". *The Educator's Room.* Retrieved July 10, 2020, from https://theeducatorsroom.com/gotta-maslow-bloom-2/

Muacevic, A., and Adler, J. (2018). Feedback can be less stressful: Medical trainee perceptions of using the Prepare to ADAPT (Ask-Discuss-Ask-Plan Together) Framework. *Cureus, 10,* 12. https://doi.org/https://www.ncbi.nlm.nih.gov/pmc/articles/PMC6428363/

Oxford English Dictionary. (2024). https://www.oed.com/ Accessed 14 March 2024.

Paris, D., and Alim, H. S. (Eds.). (2017). *Culturally sustaining pedagogies: Teaching and learning for justice in a changing world.* New York, NY: Teachers College Press.

Rist, R. C. (1972). Planned incapacitation: A case study of how not to teach black teachers to teach. *Journal of Higher Education, 43,* 620–35. doi:10.2307/1980839

Shor, I. (1993). Education in Politics. In P. McLaren and P. Leonard (Eds.), *Paulo Freire: A critical encounter.* New York: NY: Routledge.

Villegas, A. M., and Lucas, T. (2002). *Educating culturally responsive teachers.* Albany: State University of New York Press.

Weiner, L. (2003). Why is classroom management so vexing to urban teachers? *Theory into Practice, 42,* 305–12. doi:.1353/tip.2003.0052

———. (2006). Challenging deficit thinking. *Educational Leadership, 64*(1), 42–45.

Weinstein, C. S., Tomlinson-Clarke, S., and Curran, M. (2004). Toward a conception of culturally responsive classroom management. *Journal of Teacher Education, 55*(1), 25–38. doi:10.1177/0022487103259812

Wiggins, G. P., and McTighe, J. (2005). *Understanding by design* (2nd ed.). Alexandria, VA: Association for Supervision & Curriculum Development.

Zimmerman, M. (n.d.). *Complete the Line 2020.* Wakelet. https://wakelet.com/wake/st1N-zJILdYH0ozYOHGlAS

———. (2018) *Teaching AI: Exploring new frontiers for learning.* Washington, DC: International Society for Technology in Education.

Index

academic diversity, 34, 66, 133
accountability, 81, 129
activity outlines, 11
Act Local/Think Global themes, 29
Adaptable Teaching highlights: about, 9; Collaborative Planning strategy, 12–13; Culturally Responsive/Sustaining Teaching strategy, 18–20; Inquiry-based Learning strategy, 15–17; Using Assessment to Guide Instruction strategy, 14; Yearlong Overview strategy, 10–11
adult learners, 41
All the Same/All Unique activities, 116, 121
Altman, Samantha, 100–6
Asia Society, 60–61
assessment of lessons, 25–26, 110
assessment of students: choices in, 14, 17, 54–56, 81–83; quick options, 55, 111, 112; standards-based, 11, 148, 149; summative, 11, 14, 25, 46, 57; using LMSS for, 148, 149. *See also* Formative Assessments strategy; Planning with Feedback in Mind strategy

base groups of students, 81
beginnings of lessons, 93, 118
beliefs, 44
benchmarks, 56
Big Themes, 29–30
"Book Tasting" activity, 84, 85
Bradley, Jeff, 90, 146–54
Brooks, Hallie, 107–14

calendars, 10, 147, 155
CASEL (Collaborative for Academic, Social, and Emotional Learning), 60–61
Center for Intersectional Justice, 137
Center for Research on Teaching and Learning, 2
check-ins, 38, 131
checklists, 74
Christian, Moreno, 93–99
chunks of learning objectives, 25
class size adaptations, 59, 76, 133
class time adaptations, 49, 66, 76, 82, 99, 104, 114
classwork routines, 39
closing routines, 39–40
cohesiveness between units, 95
collaboration: about, 12–13; adaptations for varying opportunities, 28; interdisciplinary, 31; LMS used for, 150; with students, 73, 120; team planning, 26, 37, 156. *See also* group work
Collaborative for Academic, Social, and Emotional Learning (CASEL), 60–61
comment banks, 74–75
communication, 142–43
community: borrowing ideas, 156; building, 116; sharing toolbox with, 8, 160. *See also* collaboration
conferences with students, 40
Connecting Skills and Content to Students' Lives and Interests strategy: about, 89, 115–23; in action, 119; adaptations, 123; benefits, 96, 132; implementing, 115–23;

meaningful content and, 37–38; stories and, 94–95, 96–97
Connecting Students with Learning Goals strategy: about, 21, 22–23, 36; in action, 41, 42; adaptations, 43; benefits, 42; implementing, 36–43
Connecting Students with Previous Learning strategy: about, 22–23, 44; in action, 48, 50; adaptations, 49; benefits, 49; implementing, 44–48
Connelly, Maureen, 2, 117
Connollly, James, 44–50
content-based themes, 31
contributors' assets and needs, 5
course standards, 10
Creating Effective Rubrics strategy: about, 51, 60; in action, 63, 67; adaptations, 66; benefits, 65; implementing, 60–65; sample materials, 68–70. *See also* rubrics
Creating Positive Classroom Climate (Connelly and Davis), 117
cross-curriculum planning, 31, 56, 96
cultural icebergs, 138
cultural responsiveness and diversity, 18–20, 43, 139–40, 159. *See also* Equity and Multiple Perspectives strategy
current event themes, 29
curricular freedom adaptations, 34, 99, 123, 144
curriculum maps, 11, 45

daily topics, 11
Davis, Jonathan Ryan, 1–2, 117
DeLorenzo, Kristin, 29–35
DeMarco, Kelly, 51, 60–70
demographics, 115
Determining Learning Goals strategy: about, 21, 24; in action, 26, 28; adaptations, 28; benefits, 27; collaboration and, 26; implementing, 24–27. *See also* learning goals; objectives
differentiation, 6, 40, 108
discussion boards, 150
dispositions-based themes, 31
diversity, 19, 32, 34, 66. *See also* cultural responsiveness and diversity; Equity and Multiple Perspectives strategy
Donley, Kristin, 146–54

early-career teachers, 22, 52, 91
elementary school adaptations, 23, 53, 91, 126
endings of lessons, 94, 120
English-language learners, 4, 35, 67
Equity and Multiple Perspectives strategy: about, 90, 136; in action, 143, 145; adaptations, 144; benefits, 144; implementing, 136–43; LMS and, 148
Ettienne, Alisa, 90, 124–35
exemplars, 47

failure, 33
families: communicating with, 142–43; projects with, 145; questionnaires for, 137; using LMSs, 150, 151
feedback. *See* assessment of students; Planning with Feedback in Mind strategy
flexibility, 7, 28
flow of stories, 97
Formative Assessments strategy: about, 51, 54; in action, 58, 59; adaptations, 56–57, 58, 59; benefits, 58; implementing, 54–57
Freire, Paulo, 129

Gallery Walk, 116
games for learning, 80
gender/sexual diversity, 140, 143
getting-to-know-you activities, 117, 124, 136–41. *See also* Connecting Skills and Content to Students' Lives and Interests strategy; knowlege, skills, and dispositions (K/S/D) of students
gifted and talented programs, 4, 41
Glow statements, 61, 69
goals. *See* Connecting Students with Learning Goals strategy; Determining Learning Goals strategy; learning goals
grade level adaptations, 23, 53, 91, 126
Great School Partnership, 6
greetings, 19. *See also* getting-to-know-you activities
grid activities, 116
Groupings strategy: about, 90, 124–35; adaptations, 133; implementing, 124–35; sample materials, 135
group work: final products reflecting, 17; intentional groupings, 124–32; peer characterizations in, 134; random

groupings, 126; roles and dynamics, 129; student choice in, 81; student motivation levels in, 125–26; transitions to and from, 39
Grow statements, 61, 69
guiding questions, 23, 53, 92

Hahne, Elyse, 54–59
Heritage Dolls project, 145
high school adaptations, 23, 53, 91, 126

identity mapping, 137
inclusivity, 126, 141–43
Incorporating Routines into Your Plans strategy: about, 89, 100; in action, 104, 112; benefits, 113; implementing, 100–6; sample materials, 106
individual accountability, 81
injustices, taking action against, 20
Inquiry-based Learning, 15–17
instructions, 131–32
intentional groupings, 132
interactive modeling, 102
interdisciplinary content, 31, 35, 96
intersectionality, 137
introductions of activity/project, 16

jigsaw activities, 142
Jones, Lianne, 24–28
journals, 156

Kahoot games, 42
knowledge, skills, and dispositions (K/S/D) of students: as focus of planning, 14, 24, 25, 45; Must-Have materials and, 79–80; rubrics for, 60–61; students thinking about, 45; themes connected to, 31. *See also* Connecting Skills and Content to Students' Lives and Interests strategy
Koekemoer, Amanda, 51, 79–87

language diversity, 139
language use, 102
learning agendas, 40
Learning Cycles, 111, 116
learning goals: end-of-year, 10; feedback connecting to, 73–74; identifying, 71; overarching, 24–28; rubrics connecting to, 61; stories and, 94–96; themes and, 30. *See also* assessment of lessons; Connecting Students with Learning Goals strategy; Determining Learning Goals strategy; objectives; understanding by design (UbD)
Learning Management Systems (LMSs) strategy: about, 90, 146; in action, 152, 154; adaptations, 153; benefits, 153; implementing, 146–51; sample materials, 154
learning paths, 14
Lesson Pacing strategy: about, 89, 106, 107, 111; in action, 121, 127; adaptations, 114; benefits, 122; Getting-to-Know-You activities, 116; implementing, 107–10
lesson time. *See* class time adaptations
leveled readings, 40
LGBTQ unit, 143
literature circles, 84
LMSs. *See* Learning Management Systems (LMSs) strategy

mandated curriculum, 34
Mazor, Akiko, 90, 136–45
McTighe, Jay, 33, 42
Meet Your Students Where They Are materials, 79
middle school adaptations, 23, 53, 91, 126
middles of lessons, 93–94, 119
mini-quizzes, 112
MIP (most important point), 45–46, 48
mistakes, 33, 73–74
modeling technique, 102
modes of assessment, 14, 15
most important point (MIP), 45–46, 48
motivation in groups, 125–26
Muse, Naeem, 19
Must-Have materials, 79–80

neuro diversity, 139
New Jersey Student Learning Standards (NJSLSA), 63
Next Steps Organizers, 75
NJSLSA (New Jersey Student Learning Standards), 63
note-taking routines, 39
novel activities, 109–10

objectives: brainstorming themes for, 10; clarifying to students, 37; connecting assessment to, 14, 82, 83; state/district/school curriculum and, 24. *See also* Determining Learning Goals strategy; learning goals
O'Meally, Shellyann, 60–70
open-ended problems, 15–16
opening routines, 38
Oppici, Susan, 79–87
organization, 156

pacing of lessons. *See* Lesson Pacing strategy
peer feedback, 72
peer reviews, 65
personalization of lessons. *See* Connecting Skills and Content to Students' Lives and Interests strategy; Connecting Students with Previous Learning strategy; knowledge, skills, and dispositions (K/S/D) of students; Story of Your Lesson strategy
perspectives. *See* Equity and Multiple Perspectives strategy
photos, 119-21
physical diversity, 139
planning time adaptations, 99
Planning with Feedback in Mind strategy: about, 51, 71; in action, 75, 77; adaptations, 76; benefits, 76; for groups, 130; implementing, 71–75; sample materials, 78
practice, 160
preassessments, 44, 60
presentations, 39, 69, 120
prior learning. *See* Connecting Students with Previous Learning strategy
problem-solving toolkit, 46–47
Problem-Solving Workshop, 105

questionnaires, 136–37
questions, encouraging, 32

Radostits, Kimberly, 116, 121, 115–23
random groups, 126
real world applications, 25, 130
reflection, 17, 46, 73, 102, 135, 159
relationship building, 18

religious diversity, 140–41
resources and materials: for feedback, 74–75; identifying in planning, 15; online choices, 80; reliability of, 59
rhythm of stories, 95
Rippeteau, Heather, 89, 93–99
role assignment, 128
routines: about, 38–40; flexible *vs.* fixed elements, 101; intentionality in, 99; maintaining and extending, 101; pacing and, 107, 109; Problem-Solving Workshop, 105; in stories, 95. *See also* Incorporating Routines into Your Plans strategy
Row, Nita Luthria, 89, 115–23
rubrics: assessing with, 62–63; formats of, 62; providing feedback, 72; samples, 68, 69; student input on, 64–65. *See also* Creating Effective Rubrics strategy

safe spaces, 31–32
Sauer, Thomas, 77
Saunders, Chris, 21, 36–43
scaffolding process, 6, 16, 45–46, 147–48
school breaks, 155–56
Scupp-Jorge, Rachel, 136–45
self-assessment for students, 83
SEL (social emotional learning) tools, 47
sequencing of lessons, 95, 108
sexual/gender diversity, 140, 143
shared work: collaboration, 13; debriefing with, 16; feedback during, 74; toolbox community, 8, 160
Shor, Ira, 129
simplicity in planning, 155
SMART goals, 25
social emotional learning (SEL) tools, 47
socioeconomic diversity, 140
special education programs, 4, 28, 99
standards: aligning assessments to, 11, 148, 149; brainstorming with, 10; LMSs and, 148, 149; Must-Haves and, 79; NJSLSA, 63; in rubric development, 60–61
Stigliano, Kathleen, 36–43
Story of Your Lesson strategy: about, 89, 93; in action, 95, 98, 101, 105; adaptations, 105; benefits, 96, 99; implementing, 93–98; pacing and, 108

Student Choice strategy: about, 51, 79; in action, 84, 86; adaptations for, 85; benefits, 85; implementing, 79–83; sample materials, 86–87
Student Generated Gallery Walk, 116
Student Interest Forms, 117
students: adaptations for personality differences, 85; adapting rubrics for, 62–63, 64–65, 67; connecting with, 36–38; encouraging questions from, 32; getting to know, 117; in groups, 126, 130–31; interests, strengths, and growth areas, 30, 32; providing choices to, 40; reflections of, 73. *See also* knowledge, skills, and dispositions (K/S/D) of students; Student Choice strategy
summative assessments, 11, 14, 25, 46, 57
Summers, Margaret, 100–6
support teachers, 28

teachers' personalities, 104
Teaching for Tolerance, 60–61
team planning, 156
technology adaptations, 43, 49, 59, 85, 153
templates, 47
test reviews, 39
Thematic Planning strategy: about, 21, 22–23, 29; in action, 33; adaptations, 34; benefits, 34; implementing, 29–35, 147
time management, 157
timing of lessons, 30, 155–56. *See also* class time adaptations; Lesson Pacing strategy

Tixier, Eleanor, 44–50
To-Do List, 112
tokenism, 139
toolbox sharing community, 8, 160
toolkits for students, 46–47, 48
transitions to group/independent work, 39
trivia test review, 42

UbD (understanding by design), 6–7, 10, 33, 42, 60–64
UDL (universal design for learning), 6–7
understanding by design (UbD), 6–7, 10, 33, 42, 60–64
unit themes, 30
universal design for learning (UDL), 6–7
Unterburger, Erica, 51, 54–59
Using Assessment to Guide Instruction strategy, 14

veteran teachers, 22, 52, 91
visuals, 101
VSEPR model, 112

Wassel, Jean, 21, 24–28
Weck, Heather, 89, 107–14
weekly plans, 157
"we messages," 20
Wiggins, Grant, 6, 8, 33, 42
Workman, Emily, 21, 29–35, 89

Zimmerman, Michelle, 124–35

www.ingramcontent.com/pod-product-compliance
Lightning Source LLC
Chambersburg PA
CBHW060513300426
44112CB00017B/2652